Weatherman Walking

I/ Dylan

cofion

Derek

Weatherman Walking

Derek Brockway
and Julian Carey

Based on the BBC Wales
Radio and Television series Weatherman Walking

Published by Y Lolfa with the permission of the BBC

All maps reproduced by permission of Ordnance Survey
on behalf of HMSO. © Crown copyright 2006. All rights
reserved. Ordnance Survey Licence Number 100046541

Photographs by Julian Carey, except:

extra photographs for Cwm Cynfal by Dafydd Saer;
Elan Valley walk courtesy of Dŵr Cymru
and Elan Valley Countryside Ranger Service;
Skirrid and Llanthony Abbey walks courtesy of Chris Barber;
Llangorse Lake walk courtesy of Mike Scruby;
Kenfig Dunes walk courtesy of Graham Holmes;
Blorenge Walk courtesy of Fiona Ford and Torfaen County
Borough Council

Cover design: Y Lolfa

ISBN: 0 86243 917 5
ISBN-13 9780862439170

Printed on acid-free and partly recycled paper
and published and bound in Wales by
Y Lolfa Cyf., Talybont, Ceredigion SY24 5AP
e-mail ylolfa@ylolfa.com
website www.ylolfa.com
tel 01970 832 304
fax 832 782

Acknowledgements

So many people helped us on our walks across Wales. My thanks
to the guides for sharing their knowledge; to Julian Carey for his
energy and enthusiasm even on the wet days; the camera crew and
production team for their patience and dedication, and to Christina
Macaulay, our executive producer; to Clare Hudson and Martyn
Ingram from BBC Wales for commissioning the programme and to
my editors, Gail Morris Jones and Julie Barton, for allowing me to
go filming and take a break from my forecasting duties; to Dafydd
Saer of Y Lolfa; also to the Met Office for their support – and a big
thank you to Penny Arnold who first came up with the idea of a
radio series called *Weatherman Walking*.

Derek Brockway

Contents

Foreword

Over the past four years, I've been getting out and about across Wales in all weathers and seasons for my Radio Wales series *Weatherman Walking* and then a BBC Wales TV series of the same name. Although I've always enjoyed walking, it's been a completely different experience doing it for work. Firstly, I've had the pleasure of the company of a local expert on each walk, who has been able to point out many of the interesting features along the way. For this book, each of them has contributed a brief introduction to 'their' walk. Also alongside me has been the camera crew and producer Julian Carey who has cajoled me along through rain and shine and whose contribution to the book has been invaluable. I hope that together we can give you a flavour of some of the best walks in Wales – enjoy!

Introduction

Wales is made for walking. The landscape provides everything you could possibly wish for in terms of a walking experience – from dramatic coastal paths to shady woodland walks, wide open spaces, breathtaking mountain passes and gentle, get-away-from-it-all pockets of peace and calm – all relatively close at hand.

Wherever you find yourself in Wales, you're close to a great walk. It's a fact not lost on the rest of the country, and a quick tour of the honeypot sites will reveal walkers from all over Britain. What you'll often struggle to find is an equivalent number of home-grown ramblers on the same routes. Maybe we're just blasé about the blessings we have on our doorsteps, but the fact is, we could use and enjoy our countryside far more than we do at the moment.

Weatherman Walking is designed to make walking more attractive and get people putting their boots on and getting the benefits of this beautiful country. For a start, you don't have to be a super-fit outdoors type to tackle some of these really rewarding paths and little-known routes around Wales. Yes, you do have to be sensible, follow some basic rules, and be properly dressed. But there are thousands of miles of incredible walks – all for free – which will make you feel fitter and better, and will lift your spirits.

Walking is now one of the most popular pastimes in Britain, and it's something that you can spend a lifetime doing. When we were filming in Cordell Country, between Blaenavon and Bryn-mawr, we ran into a man celebrating his 92nd birthday by taking a walk along an abandoned tram line – a line he remembered being in use when he was a child. Togged out in state-of-the-art walking shoes and a bright Gor-Tex coat, he walked a couple of times a week on various routes all over South Wales and Herefordshire.

If he can do it – then why not you?

And that's the final point. Walking is an activity that can be enjoyed by all the family. From grandparents to grandchildren, everyone can walk the right route at the same time and enjoy the experience together. And how many activities are there that you can say that about?

Getting started

OK, let's admit it – people have accidents in the mountains and waters around Wales. Some of them are serious, but they are rare in relation to the number of people using the landscape. As long as you take care, do a little preparation and are realistic about your ability, then you should be fine. For example, recognise your limits. Ask yourself – how fit are you? Are you experienced enough to undertake a particular walk? And what about the people you're walking with? Are they up to the route you've chosen? If you can't answer those questions with certainty, then choose another walk – an easier one. The point is to get out there and enjoy yourself. It's not about putting yourself and others in difficulty and danger.

The best way to start walking is to join a group. Most of the National Parks offer a series of guided walks throughout the year, and a quick flick through your local paper or community website should reveal a walking group near you. They're a great, safe way to enjoy the countryside and to meet people – after all, Wordsworth might have 'wandered lonely as a cloud', but there's no reason why you have to. If nothing else, it gives you the chance to swap all your dodgy sandwiches!

A guided walk means you'll have someone on hand to steer you safely along, and help you get the most out of the day. They can point out the wildlife, read the landscape for clues about the past, and pass on tips and skills that will allow you to stretch out on your own.

Most National Parks also offer map reading courses and supply loads of helpful leaflets and maps. Even with this excellent book by your side, you are advised to check with them before you start exploring. They know best and will help you make the right decisions.

A walking wardrobe

One piece of advice you really must take is to get the right equipment. The most common accident is a simple slip, so getting kitted out with the right footwear is the first place to start. Your boots should have a suitable tread – and, just like the tyres on your car, if that tread is worn or not up to the job, then you'll soon be in trouble. Old boots may be comfortable, but they're useless if they don't grip properly, particularly in wet conditions.

Also, you need shoes with ankle support. On rough terrain, anyone can turn an ankle, regardless of age or fitness, and a boot with properly-fitted support will reduce the chance of that happening. Finally, you don't want to end up with blisters, so don't totally abandon the idea of comfort! Wear your shoes in gently, and get some proper walking socks to keep your feet dry and protected from rubbing.

Luckily, there are dozens of appropriate shoes on the market, and a decent shoe specialist can advise you on what you should be wearing, but give them plenty of information about the kind of walking you intend to do, and about your own level of fitness and experience.

As for covering the rest of you, warm, windproof and waterproof clothing is essential. You should always think about taking a small rucksack too, so you can pack extra layers as well as your food and drink. For example, a hat, gloves and waterproofs should always be carried as well as an extra layer. Some people take a small groundsheet with them too. Why? Well, say the weather does turn nasty, or you do end up taking a tumble, you'll need to keep warm and dry until you can be picked up, or the clouds go away. If you're prepared, you'll probably never need it. And the groundsheet means you have something dry to sit on when you bring out the flask of tea and the biscuits.

Which brings us to your provisions. Always take more than you need – even if it's only an extra apple or bar of chocolate. The Welsh countryside is beautiful, but it lacks corner shops and coffee bars, so bring your own! Also, in cold weather it's important to carry a hot drink and high-energy food. And make sure everyone in your group has enough – that way you'll be safe, you'll enjoy your time more, and there'll be no squabbling over the last biscuit!

Finally, pack a first-aid kit, a torch, a whistle, and – if you can afford one – a survival bag (it's a sort of mini tent-cum-sleeping bag). You may never have to use any of them, but you'll thank your lucky stars you packed them if you ever do.

One last point – mobile phones. Sometimes you'll be surprised at where you will get a signal; at other times you'll be astonished at the lack of reception. The bottom line is, take them but don't rely on them; let people know where you're going and when you expect to be back. And of course, when you do arrive back, let them know you've returned safely – otherwise there'll be an unnecessary panic.

Does that all sound scary? Probably. But don't be put off. It's better to be safe than sorry. So plan for the worst, even though it's unlikely ever to happen.

Welsh weather

Do we have to mention the fact that the weather in Wales is very changeable? Well, maybe it's worth stressing that, when you're out in the countryside, those changes happen faster and are more dramatic, and you have little or no opportunity to avoid them.

The thing to do is to check your specialist weather forecasts carefully. The major National Parks and tourist centres are a good place for information, as are local forecasts such as the Radio Wales bulletins and hill forecasts – and of course there's the BBC website, www.bbc.co.uk/walesweather. But as a general rule of thumb, remember that the higher you climb, the colder it gets, and the stronger the wind gets.

Also, beware of stiff sea breezes on sunny days – when we were filming in Pembrokeshire, looking for dolphins near Bardsey Island, some of the crew came away with sunburnt faces. It didn't feel hot, but the combination of the wind and the sun did a lot of damage. So pack some sunblock and lip salve in that rucksack too!

One final word about the weather: the best piece of advice is to be prepared to change your plans if things turn nasty. Make sure everyone understands that the best route is the one that brings everyone back safely and brings them back happy.

When you plan your walk, plan according to the weather forecast. Think of alternatives if the weather is bad, and prepare a route that allows a quick get-out if necessary (something which is particularly important if you're taking children with you or if there are elderly walkers in the party).

Off you go

If you've taken all that advice on board, what you should do next is get out there and start walking. The TV series Weatherman Walking featured eight walks in four seasons – and just one Derek Brockway!

We've taken each of those walks and presented them here, together with an extra walk for each season drawn from Derek's BBC Radio Wales series of the same name. These are walks for all kinds of abilities, and even the difficult or really long ones can be broken down into easier, more foot-friendly rambles. Many of them are offered as guided walks by the various authorities that look after the sites, such as the National Trust. And the golden rule is to check with them first before tackling the paths – they have all the best advice and up-to-date information to hand.

Julian Carey
Weatherman Walking Producer, BBC Wales

Autumn

Cwm Cynfal, Snowdonia

Near: Blaenau Ffestiniog

Ordnance Survey Grid Reference SH 701419

Derek says...

This is a stunning walk through woodland to the dramatic Cynfal Falls or Rhaeadr Cynfal and is only a stone's throw from the village of Llan Ffestiniog. It is a great walk in late Autumn when the leaves are changing colour.

There really is a magical feel about this place, especially on a misty October morning, with strange giant mushrooms growing up along the path. It's easy to imagine how the legendary exorcist and mystic Huw Llwyd cast a spell over the local congregation.

This is a unique environment: many of the plants found here can only survive where these ancient trees lock in the moisture-laden atmosphere of the river gorge. I just love the ferns and the luscious green mosses that thrive in the moist air, carpet the river banks and cover the trees.

The sound of the river thundering its way through the gorge is amazing but it is also a very peaceful walk with only the odd stray hoot from the Blaenau Ffestiniog train to interrupt the birdsong and waterfalls cascading their way down the valley.

An intermediate walk, about a four-mile round trip from the village of Llan Ffestiniog. Dramatic in all weathers but at its very best after rain has filled the cataracts. You will need waterproofs in wet weather and mind the slippery stone steps and bridge crossing the river.

This gorge is one of those magical places that will not let you forget its dramatic waterfalls, Rhaeadr Ddu and Rhaeadr Cynfal, and Huw Llwyd's Pulpit, that strange rock pillar in the river. Huw Llwyd was an early 17th-century soldier, whose writings on military strategy were studied by Napoleon Bonaparte. He was also a renowned poet and healer, though more of a magician than physician in his methods! He would baptise people in the river and, from above in his 'Pulpit', would cast out his patients' demons and hurl them to the oblivion below!

Twm Elias
Plas Tan-y-Bwlch Environmental Studies Centre

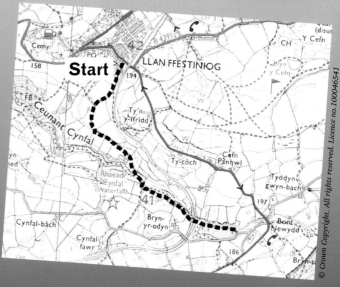

Derek and Twm looking for direction – not from a map and compass, but from the camerman!

The Moelwyn mountains rising above Llan Ffestiniog

You don't have to undertake gravity-defying feats of endurance to find a rewarding walk in Snowdonia. The area is a honeypot of fabulous paths, with plenty to offer everyone from hardcore walkers to first-time ramblers.

But away from the 'Hollywood trails' that always hog the headlines, there are some hidden gems that offer more bang for your walking buck. One of the best is at Cwm Cynfal. It's arguably one of the area's oldest attractions, with people travelling from all over Europe to visit this magical place as far back as the seventeenth century. They came to congregate at the infamous Rhaeadr Du (the Black Falls) although, back then, it wasn't exercise that lured them here – it was exorcism!

In those days, the beautiful woods and river gorge were the haunt of Huw Llwyd, a powerful Welsh magician – or, depending on your point of view, a particularly clued-up medicine man and former mercenary! He found an ingenious use for the stunning waterfalls and the treacherous cataracts that rise from the gorge with spooky malevolence. But more of him later…

You see, it wasn't just faith healers who flocked to Cwm Cynfal. Long after Huw had spirited himself away, the area became popular with Victorian walkers who were quick to spot the potential of the waterfalls and the stunning scenery. Local hoteliers and businessmen built bridges and put a basic infrastructure into place so that more people could enjoy the river and gorge and visit the area. In fact, if you keep your eyes peeled in the latter stages of the walk, you'll spot rusty steel cables strung from tree to tree – the remnants of a crude system of safety barriers, an early attempt to stop the intrepid visitors sliding down into the water below.

A hundred years or so later, this great little walk is not so well-known and more often than not is missed by modern walkers – which is a real shame. It's a great beginners' walk: gentle, mostly downhill, just two miles long, and with some stunning scenery. Not only that, but it starts right in the heart of the little hamlet of Llan Ffestiniog and is book-ended by easy parking places.

The village church at Llan Ffestiniog

You can start the walk from the centre of the village, outside the church and the local pub, the Pengwern Arms. A long-established rendezvous point, Llan Ffestiniog was well known to the drovers who used to meet here on their way to England over 150 years ago. These days it's hard to imagine the sleepy village teeming with cattle and Welsh cowboys – although it's hardly remote. The A470 runs right through it, and as it lies just south of the famous slate town of Blaenau Ffestiniog, it makes for a very accessible walk.

From the pub car park you head up the main road, passing the village school and turning off to your right, before the railway bridge. Ducking past the slate slab fences of the sheep pens – a higgledy-piggledy tombstone trail that leads you in and out of a local farm – the path soon opens up onto the rolling hills behind the village.

Down through the fields, the walk is clearly signposted and keeps you safely attached to the dry stone wall that clings to the slopes of the valley. Here, parts of the walk overlook a steep slide to the river, although it shouldn't prove difficult even for inexperienced walkers.

The first third of the walk is all open scenery – a typical Welsh country farm walk with opportunities to see circling ravens overhead, collared doves and birds of prey, as well as evidence of an active set of badgers and other wildlife. You also get some spectacular views of the Moelwyn Mountains that loom large behind the village church steeple.

However, the real treats begin when you cross from the grazing fields and pasture to the Cynfal Forest, a site of special scientific interest,

maintained by the Countryside Commission for Wales. Once inside the forest, the paths are more clearly defined. There's also an information board guiding you around the various waterfalls and features of the gorge, explaining the scientific importance of the area. It's a unique environment. The combination of a deep, narrow gorge and a series of waterfalls surrounded by a mature forest means that a lot of the atmospheric moisture generated by the river is trapped beneath the tree canopy. As a result it is a haven for mosses, liverworts and lichens. Spectacular ferns erupt from the branches overhead, tree trunks are coated in fine, soft mosses, and even the dry stone walls are carpeted in rich green fur. It's a luscious landscape, and with the thundering water in the background and the chatter of birds in the trees, you feel as if you're in a vibrant, magical forest, bursting with life and energy. The trees also filter the sunlight through the gorge, adding to the air of otherworldliness and casting criss-cross patterns over the exposed rock faces of the latter stages of the trail.

On entering the forest you're immediately drawn down to the first of several spectacular features – the Black Falls or Rhaeadr Du. Thick, chunky stone steps lead down to a railing-fenced viewing platform that offers a dramatic view of the falls – although they can get wet and slippery, so take care.

The falls get their name from the lichen that lives on the rock; it turns black when wet, giving the location an obsidian sheen, 365 days of the year. If you're lucky enough to see the falls after a rainstorm (while at the same time hopefully avoiding any rainfall yourself!) then the platform gives you a real sense of the water's power and violence. The danger of those black waters was part of the attraction of the gorge to old Huw Llwyd. There are many folk tales about the famous wizard, and while most of those seem fantastical, there's no doubt that he did exist.

A native of the area, he was born around 1580 and travelled to the continent to earn his fortune as a mercenary. He fought all over Europe in various feudal conflicts, and even wrote a book about warfare and military tactics. But Huw wasn't just a fighter; he was also a skilful poet and something of an amateur scientist and astrologer.

When he finally came home from his adventures abroad, he returned with an extensive knowledge of medicinal plants and herbs, as well as a flair for showmanship and crowd psychology. He set himself up as a magician and wise man, with a fierce reputation as someone who was handy with a sword and also adept at various murky black arts. That reputation not only kept him and his fortune safe at his farm in the valley, but it also had another unexpected side effect. As his fame spread, people from all over Britain and Europe travelled to the Cynfal Forest to seek help from Huw – who now had a burgeoning practice as an exorcist and medicine man extraordinaire. For a fee, he would take these troubled souls down to the river, and 'cure' them at a spot which has since become known as 'Huw Llwyd's Pulpit'. It still survives to this day, and is the very next feature that we find on the walk.

Huw Llwyd's Pulpit seen from two different angles

Rising from the centre of the river, the pulpit is a 12-foot-high rock tower overlooking a man-size slab below, laid out like a sacrificial altar. Taking these two naturally-occurring features, Huw fashioned a routine to dazzle his congregation. The afflicted soul (who was no doubt treated beforehand with various roots and herbs) would be taken down to the waters and told to lie on the slab. Then Huw would climb the tower and, in full magician's regalia, with cloak, staff and spell book, he would begin to holler and howl and 'cast out' the evil forces possessing the terrified 'patient' below.

After a prolonged and hysterical performance, he would announce that he had taken hold of the evil spirits and cast them into the waters where they were swept away and dashed on the rocks at the Black Falls below. One imagines that few argued with this version of events or with

Fungus – one of the few things you'll find growing down on the ground under the conifers

his method of healing – and few were brave enough to ask for a second opinion (or indeed give one).

The walk today offers a fantastic view from above the Pulpit, although if the thought of looking down onto the jagged slabs and swirling waters twenty feet below has you feeling dizzy, don't worry. There's another route slightly higher up which still affords a good view of Huw's former workplace, but is less likely to provoke an attack of vertigo!

Walkers are advised not to try and beat a path down to the foot of the pulpit and the slab itself. It's a steep drop and very wet terrain. One wrong move and Huw Llwyd would be the least of your troubles.

Another important point to bear in mind is that the whole area around the Pulpit is rich in rare and delicate plant life. The forest boasts some of the best examples of mosses and lichen in the whole of north-western Europe, encouraged by the relatively mild climate and high rainfall. Typically, these botanical riches occur most frequently in the more inaccessible areas, and unfortunately are only of significance to the trained eye. The untrained eye can still enjoy the environment, though, as the mixture of lichens and mosses create a range of beautiful patterns and mosaics that colour the carpet of the forest floor, as well as the decaying tree branches, rocks and outcrops. And they're not just pretty to look at: during the First World War, for example, sphagnum moss was harvested by locals and sent to the front where it was used as wound dressing in the absence of cotton wool. If you spot some, try squeezing it and see just how much water comes dribbling out – it's like a little green sponge!

There are banks of this highly absorbent plant just beyond the footbridge that takes you across the river, as the walk winds itself across to the furthest bank for its final stages. This is where you'll catch sight of the rusting cables as the path climbs up to the spectacular conclusion of the walk and the main Cynfal Falls. Standing over 25 feet high, the towering cascade of water feeds a series of sheltered pools which will have walkers scrabbling for their cameras.

The trail offers a number of good vantage points, and it's worth taking

your time and soaking up the atmosphere at these beautiful falls. As water features go, it takes some beating! The view was featured on a popular picture postcard back in the early 1900s and originals frequently crop up at collectors fairs and on e-Bay. If you track one down, you'll see that the area is virtually unchanged and would probably still be familiar to old Huw Llwyd, should he ever reappear.

Although the Falls are the natural climax to the walk, the path continues on for another half a mile, winding under a high stone railway bridge and through a collection of twisted, moss-covered trees, all soundtracked by the gentle babble of the river. It's a fantasy landscape that your mind – as well as your feet – can wander through.

The final fifteen metres of the walk soon brings you back to earth, however, as the path takes you over a green moss-carpeted stone wall and stile, and into the dry pine-covered floor of a conifer plantation. The contrast between the vibrant, lush eco-system of Nant Cynfal and the shadowy environment of the managed Forestry Commission land is a shock to the system. It also shows just how important it is to preserve the few ancient woodlands that remain in Wales.

A quick sidestep through pine columns and you hit the main road. The lazy walker will have had the foresight to either park a second car here or arrange to be picked up. Those made of hardier stock will simply turn back at the stile and follow the path back to the village, enjoying a different perspective on the walk and using up what's left of the film in their cameras.

Craig-y-Nos

Near: Neath

Ordnance Survey Grid Reference SN 839155

OS Explorer Map OL12

Derek says...

This walk is a little more challenging than some of the others but worth the effort, even on a wet day in autumn. The landscape may appear bleak and yet is dramatic and beautiful. The most interesting part is wandering through the limestone terrain with its jagged rocks and shake holes.

You are exposed to the elements on this walk and should come prepared. The weather can change quickly. We encountered a thunderstorm and although I enjoy watching a good storm from my bedroom window it's a different matter on the side of a mountain. I must admit to being slightly scared and told everyone to take cover. We sheltered amongst rocks using an emergency tent which I called an inflatable Wendy house! The storm was short but the helicopter hired to take aerial photographs suffered minor damage to its tail wing caused by gusty winds. Thankfully we survived in one piece and continued on to the crash site of the Wellington bomber where we paid our respects.

This is a great walk and if you have time, take a look around Craig-y-Nos Country Park; it is lovely in autumn when the leaves are turning orange and rusty red.

This walk has spiritual qualities as well as its fascinating natural landmarks: the quirky limestone features, those streams that just disappear into holes in the ground, and the pockmarking of the shake holes scattered across the hills.

This is the land of legends: we pass the sleeping giant, who will awaken should the nation be in peril. The wide open spaces which, according to the Mabinogion, once echoed with the squeals of the Twrch Trwyth and his cohort of piglets as they were chased by Culhwch and some of King Arthur's knights.

But the walk also has a poignant aspect. At the site of the crashed Wellington bomber, I am always saddened by the lives wasted on that bitter November night when the aircraft plummeted to a tragic end, killing all the young airmen on board.

However, the conservation project to green-up Waun Fignen Felen is a source of great optimism and joy. Plants are starting to grow across the vast eroding peat bog, stabilising the surface and locking in once more the secrets that the peat conceals, preserving them for future generations and lessening the impact on the cave system below.

Judith Harvey
Brecon Beacons National Park

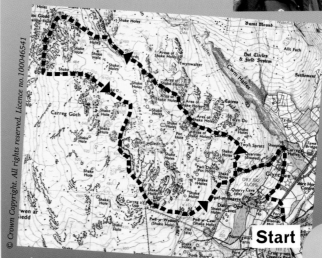

Start

25

If the first autumn walk was fairly easy going, then this one is a little bit more challenging. For a start, there's a fair bit of height to gain – and if you're not used to big uphill climbs, your thighs might start to complain after about 10 minutes!

Not only that, but if you want to walk in Derek's footsteps and find that crashed World War II bomber, then your best bet is to join one of the National Park's guided walks – or else walk with someone who is a very accomplished map reader and who knows the area well.

One other word of advice: the weather up here can change very quickly. When we filmed here, we were hit by driving rain, thick mist and a sudden thunderstorm which had us cowering under an emergency tent until it blew over. That said, the first half of the walk is fairly straightforward and delivers stunning views of Craig-y-Nos castle and the valley below – and remember, if it ever gets too wet or too tough, then you can always walk around the gardens at Craig-y-Nos park or pop into the caves at nearby Dan-yr-Ogof.

Start the walk from the Craig-y-Nos visitor centre. It's a good place to check on the weather for the day, and it also gives you the chance to swot up on the area's history and wildlife.

Crossing the main road, you head past the ponies and llamas at Dan-yr-Ogof's lower car park and then follow the signs for the public footpath that leads you onto the mountain. From there the only way is up, first through a kissing gate and then onto a route that runs alongside the river Tawe, which should interest any amateur geologists as it marks the dividing line between the limestone and the red sandstone. It's the presence of the limestone which creates the spectacular caves down below, as well as the mind-boggling array of shake holes and geological features on top of the mountain.

As the path bends up and around you begin to get some great views of the castle, the former home of early

Derek getting suited and booted for the walk – note the plastic bags full of crisp packets stuffed in the back of his car!

operatic superstar Adelina Patti – the Madonna of her day and a woman who scandalised society back in the 1870s. Born in Spain in 1843, she was brought up in America and became the most celebrated soprano in the world, with a voice that Verdi described as the best he had ever heard. She settled in Wales with her second husband after falling in love with the wild Welsh scenery – which she soon set about landscaping to look more like the Italian mountains! She bought the castle in 1878 for £3,500 and then spent £100,000 remodelling it and doubling the size of the original building. She also had her own private railway installed and built her very own opera house within the castle walls. It's still there, and these days it's licensed for weddings, something the romantic and thrice married Madame Patti would no doubt have approved of.

Craig-y-Nos castle, former home of Adelina Patti

Viewed from the mountain path on a damp and misty autumn day, there is a fairy tale feel to the castle nestled among the trees below. In fact, the whole landscape has an ethereal, otherworldly atmosphere.

As the path meanders through the odd lumps and bumps that break out over the mountain, you can find a real sense of solitude and space, and while it can be brooding and bleak, it is no less beautiful for it. It also feels timeless. There is little here that lets you know that the mountain was ever inhabited or worked, apart from some old lime quarry workings and a kiln, some stone walls, and not much else. Even the kiln looks like a ruined Hobbit hole in the side of the hill. The lime was dug out and burned here before being used to fertilise the land. These days, the sheep are the only ones to benefit from that industry, wandering as they do all over the mountain. On our walk you could hear them calling out to one another through the low, light fog – like lost souls haunting the heather-covered moors.

It's no wonder that the team behind Doctor Who chose this place as the setting for their terrifying werewolf episode, when the countryside here doubled for the Highlands of Scotland. But if all this talk of monsters and the macabre is starting to scare you off the slopes, then maybe we should talk about the science rather than the supernatural, because the big attraction here these days are the bizarre and mind-boggling array of geological curiosities which have earned the region its status as an European Geopark.

Below ground it's the Dan-yr-Ogof showcaves that best tell the story of this area's interesting earth history. But above ground, this walk will reveal other clues to the rich geological heritage of the mountain – the most obvious being the baffling array of shake holes which pit and dimple the ground all over the mountainside. To give you an idea of just how many holes and ponds dot the landscape, have a look at the OS map for the area. From the air it looks like the surface of the moon, in that it's dotted with craters. In fact, when the pilot of the helicopter we'd hired to film the mountain looked down on the deep depressions below him he asked if the place had been used for bombing practice!

*View of the bog
at Waun Fignen Felen*

The holes are caused by erosion of the limestone underneath the earth: acid rain eats away at the rock, causing a collapse which pulls everything down into a hole. It's also the reason why so many small ponds litter the landscape, creating mini oases for insects and small animals.

The Fforest Fawr Geopark, as the area is now called, is the first internationally recognised geopark in Wales. It was awarded this status by UNESCO in 2005, becoming the 24th member of this global network of Geoparks.

In total, over 470 million years of earth history are recorded in the rocks of this western tip of the Brecon Beacons, and here they are at their most visible and spectacular. About two-thirds of the way to the bog you'll spot a rash of weird, corroded spiked stone outcrops. They look like the surface of an alien planet, but are caused by acid rain wearing away the soft limestone rock.

Throughout these strange, sharp, scarred landscapes you'll see the odd hawthorn bush gamely trying to grow, and they dot the horizon like bizarre little bonsai trees. They appear here because the scoured rock is too difficult for the sheep to get across, so they can't eat the young shoots. As such, you get a glimpse of the kind of plant life that would flourish on the mountain if the grazing animals were ever taken away.

As the path winds its way up the mountain, you may want to stop and take a breather – but consider this – a hundred years ago this was the main route between villages such as Llanddeusant and the factories and brick works of Swansea. And when workers were killed there, their bodies would be carried in coffins along this path by teams of men who would meet in the middle at the top of the mountain and swap their tragic cargo.

Mucky business! Wardens and volunteers doing the dirty work and saving the bog

Most modern walkers will only go as far as the peat bog at Waun Fignen Felen, and while it might not sound like the most spectacular of destinations it's well worth a visit. For a start, it's an incredibly important site, which the Park is working hard at restoring and protecting. Why protect a peat bog? OK, admittedly to the untrained eye it looks like a massive mud hole, but don't discount it out of hand. Waun Fignen Felen was once the site of a Mesolithic village. Back then it wasn't a bog – it was a lake, and tribes hunted and fished there. Over the centuries, the lake gradually dried out to form the bog, creating a different kind of ecosystem.

But this drying out process has accelerated over the last few hundred years, and that has started to cause real problems. As the bog becomes more eroded, the peat has begun to get washed down into the cave system below. As well as being a major tourist attraction, Dan-yr-Ogof Caves are

There are easier ways to get up the mountain ... although we never used the helicopter for transport, just for filming (so yes we really did walk all the way up here carrying our cameras and equipment!)

also a protected nature reserve, and the peat pollutes their fragile ecosystem. Also, a great deal of important material is being washed underground from the surface. The layers of peat hold pollen records going back centuries, giving vital clues to climate change in the area – but these, too, are at risk of being lost.

The park now has a programme aimed at stabilising the bog, sowing grass seed and damming the streams that run through it with great bales of hay. These act as ditch blocks to slow down the flow of water flowing through the area, helping to hydrate the bog and stop the erosion caused by the streams. And if that all seems like a lot of work to protect a big muddy mountainside, think about this: if all the peat bogs in Britain were fully hydrated and functioning, then they could sink all the carbon we have agreed to cut back on under the terms of the Kyoto Agreement.

As far as walkers are concerned, though, the most important fact about the bog is that it marks the point where most people would turn back and head for home. Walking this far would have your heart pumping and your lungs filled with fresh air. It would also give you a flavour of the mountain and a taste of the Fforest Fawr area.

However, we wanted to take in one more sight before we left the mountain. So, instead of heading straight back, we used a map and compass and left the path to cut across country and head for a truly evocative and eerie war memorial. It doesn't appear on the OS Map and is surrounded by shake holes, ponds and exposed rock face; as such it's not an easy place to find and is a slightly more difficult walk than that which leads to the bog. It's dedicated to the crew of a Wellington bomber that crashed into the mountain in November 1944. The six Canadians on board were killed when the wings of their plane iced up, and the engines failed as they flew over the mountain in the dead of night. They couldn't clear the top and crashed.

There is a permanent memorial to the airmen, but the most striking thing about the site is that the wreckage of the bomber has been left as a tribute to the young men who died that night. It is remarkably well preserved, but as it is mostly a dull silver in appearance, and is laid out more or less flat to the ground, it can be hard to spot. But when you do find the wreckage – and if it's a cold misty, miserable day, as it was when we filmed – you'll be struck by just how powerful a memorial this is. It's such an isolated, lonely place, and with the wind blowing through the poppy wreaths left here every Remembrance Sunday, you can't help but be affected by the reminders of their sacrifice.

The wreckage of a Wellington bomber which crashed in 1944

It takes about half an hour to find the crash site from the Waun Fignen Felen bog, and then your guide would take you down the mountain, through the rocky cleft known as the Goat's Castle, past ponds and even more sinkholes, to meet the main path where it once again overlooks Madam Patti's castle.

From there, it's a steady downhill walk back to the car park, but if you've time and energy left, pop into the visitor centre and check out the illustrated history of the castle and the life and times of Adelina Patti – you can even buy a CD of her collected recordings. Or go straight to the bar and tea room at the castle, and see what it looks like from ground level – just be careful you don't disturb the great lady's ghost!

Skirrid Fawr

Near: Abergavenny

Ordnance Survey Grid Reference SO 328163

OS Explorer Map OL13

Derek says...

I really enjoyed this walk and not just because there's a cosy pub at the end, although there's nothing like a pint after a day out in the hills! This short stroll is fairly easy, suitable for beginners and walkers of all ages: perfect for an autumn afternoon of family fun.

There's a great view of Sugarloaf Mountain from the top of Skirrid or Holy Mountain. On a clear day you can see as far as the Malvern Hills in England. You also get cracking views of the Black Mountains and the town of Abergavenny spread out around the river below.

If you do follow our suggested path over the mountain into the village, you get a chance to walk through gorgeous farmland and pass the peacocks who patrol the grounds at Llanvihangel Court.

Now you've earned it, quench your thirst in Wales' oldest pub. There are some gruesome stories associated with the Skirrid Inn but I never saw anything ghostly or horrible when I went in there – apart from my producer!

Skirrid Fawr is just 1595 feet but feels like a true mountain, with views towards the Sugar Loaf and the Black Mountains. Its unusual shape has given rise to many legends and superstitions. According to one, the notch on its west side was caused by the underside of Noah's ark! Another claims the ravine appeared when a bolt of lightning marked Christ's crucifixion. For this reason, the peak is also known as the Holy Mountain, while the name Skirrid is a corruption of Ysgyrydd which means 'that which has been shaken'.

Next to the trig point is a depression marking the site of a one-time Roman Catholic chapel dedicated to St Michael. Another landmark visible from the summit is the old pilgrams' destination, White Castle and its stone towers.

We traversed the Holy Mountain and made our way across farmland, passing the historic Elizabethan mansion of Llanfihangel Court, then on to the twelfth-century Skirrid Inn, reputed to be the oldest pub in Wales as well as the most haunted pub in Britain.

Chris Barber
Walking Wales Magazine

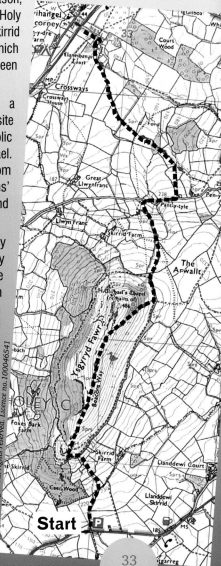

Seasoned walkers who know the Abergavenny area will raise their eyebrows at the Skirrid being put forward as an autumn walk, and in truth there are good arguments for recommending it for winter, spring and summer too.

But this book is all about encouraging people onto the hills and mountains of Wales, and on a crisp autumn day, or indeed any day that benefits from those 'Indian summers' of late September, the Skirrid makes for a great introduction to walking.

For one thing, the early steep path through Caer wood can be a bit clammy and close if you walk it on a hot summer's day – and as this section of the walk is also the steepest, you might prefer to do it in a cooler season. Not only that, but the view as you head up onto the ridge reveals the autumn colours below in the trees and farmland as well as the mountains surrounding it – like the Blorenge, Sugar Loaf and the Black Mountains.

And as a final clincher, you can end the walk in the historic Skirrid Inn, Wales's oldest and most haunted pub, and one where a cold and weary walker will find a good welcome. If you do make it there, look out for the 'hanging beam', the beam above the stairwell where criminals were executed back in times when the pub also served as a courthouse.

A pub has stood on the spot for nine centuries, and a report of a hanging there in 1110 is the first official mention of the Skirrid Inn (the unlucky miscreant was found guilty of sheep stealing before being dispatched to that great pasture in the sky). The infamous hanging judge, Judge Jeffries, held court there and one of his potential victims is alleged to haunt the pub. Legend has it that a one-eyed convict, who cheated the rope by stabbing himself to death, has been seen haunting the ladies' toilet (which a long time ago used to be the holding cell for condemned prisoners).

It's not just the pub but the whole area which is steeped in bloody history. Owain Glyndŵr rallied his troops here before marching on Pontrilas, while from the peak of the Skirrid you can see the remains of an Iron Age fort. Finally at the mountain's trig point, you can make out the outline of a Catholic church and meeting place which was torn down in the 1600s.

So you have stunning views, an easy path and bags of legends and history; it should come as no surprise, then, to learn that this is a very popular walk. It's a particular favourite with families as it's not too demanding for children, and as most people tend to make it to the top and then retrace their steps, it's easy to turn back if little ones get tired or frustrated.

If you're new to walking, then the simple 'up and down route' might be the best course of action for you to follow; but if you are fairly fit then you should consider exiting the Skirrid in the opposite direction and taking the long walk to the pub, via Llanvihangel Court towards Llanvihangel Crucorney – and the Skirrid Inn, of course. As befits a walk made for beginners, the route is easy to find and follow.

Taking the B4521 from Abergavenny you'll see a lay-by on your left hand side, just before the right turn to Bryn y Gwenyn and the famous Walnut Tree restaurant.

Go over the stile and head up a wide gravel access road until you reach another gate and stile at the entrance to the wood. The gravel is a recent addition – courtesy of the National Trust, who own the mountain, having been given it by a local landowner in 1938.

From the second stile, the path is easy to spot – a lot of walking boots have passed this way and it's easy to follow in their footsteps. Before you do, take a look back down the path. From this vantage point you'll see a conical tree-covered hill, Skirrid Fach, or Little Skirrid – and remember that you're on Skirrid Fawr, Big Skirrid.

From here on the path zig-zags through the wood, up towards a second stile, at which point you turn right and keep going up.

All that remains of the old Catholic church, two door stones and a view down the spine of the Skirrid

As you clear the tree line you'll see the ridge rising in front of you. This is one of Skirrid's playful quirks: as you climb the ridge, the spine above it reveals itself quite slowly and secretively. So you may think you've hit the top but, in truth, there's another half mile or so of broken, rising terrain before you hit the trig point on the summit. Also, the wind can whip around here too, so even if you pick a sunny autumn day to tackle the Skirrid, remember to carry a coat or warmer clothing in your backpack. You'll want to stop along the way and admire the views, so be prepared and make sure your body doesn't cool down too quickly while you stand around taking photographs of the spectacular scenery.

The spine of the Skirrid is about 50 feet wide and it allows magnificent views of eastern Monmouthshire, and even the Malverns on your right hand side, and the Black Mountains, Blorenge and Sugar Loaf on the left. The Blorenge is dealt with in our winter walks section and, together with the Sugar Loaf and Skirrid, it makes up the three peaks of Abergavenny (and yes – there's a popular annual walk which challenges people to tackle all three summits in one day).

As for the Sugar Loaf, it's easy to spot; it got its name from its distinctive shape which is reckoned to look like a pile of sugar poured straight from the bag (it also looks vaguely like a benign green volcano!). Its original name is Mynydd Pen-y-Fâl, and it's separated from the Black Mountains by the Grwyne Fawr valley.

In the 1880s, Buffalo Bill brought his Wild West show to Abergavenny, and the sight of the Sugar Loaf so inspired the famous cowboy that he vowed onstage to walk to the top of it the day after the show. He did so, and half the town – it's said – went with him. It's not known if he ever scaled the Skirrid too, but a stone on the ridge proves that someone was hiking up there in 1890. The date is one of many carved into the huge stone by walkers at the turn of the last century. Unlike today, it seems a staple part of a Victorian walker's kit was a hammer and chisel and, although acid rain has now worn away a lot of the messages, a few names have survived. Hopefully, modern-day walkers will continue to ignore this old tradition and keep the summit free of graffiti!

As the gradual ascent to the trig point continues, look out to the right over the patchwork quilt of farmland and try and spot the towers of White Castle – one of three castles in the area (the others being Grosmont and Skenfrith). Built to control the Welsh, the castle was rebuilt in the 13th century by Hubert de Burgh, although a fortress had occupied the site for much longer. The Skirrid can boast its own Iron Age hill fort, although it's better viewed from the Llanvihangel side of the mountain.

It's easier to spot the remains – such as they are – of St Michael's Church, the small Catholic refuge that

Llanfihangel Court

used to crown the summit. Just two stones which mark the entrance to the church are all that survived the building's destruction in 1678.

You can make out the square outline of the little church, and a painting of the mountain with St Michael still intact can be seen in Llanvihangel Court. Churches dedicated to St Michael are often found in high places – one stood at the top of Glastonbury Tor – and at 1,594 feet above sea level, the top of the Skirrid should have kept Catholics safe while they worshipped here during the period of religious persecution in Wales. The church is one of the reasons why the Skirrid is known as the Holy Mountain. The other reasons are all to do with its bizarre shape. It was caused by an ancient landslide, although local folklore has provided three alternative stories to explain its broken-backed profile.

One claims that the bow of Noah's Ark was to blame as it brushed the top of the mountain during the deluge and drove a passage through the peak. Another story would have you believe that the Skirrid was cracked open by a bolt of lightning, unleashed in God's fury at Jesus's crucifixion. The third story has some biblical connotation too – in that the devil is supposed to have sat on the Skirrid taking a break from purgatory and damnation before the giant Jack of Kent came crashing in. Jack was jumping across the valley from the Sugar Loaf, and the imprint of the heel of his boot is supposed to have formed the ravine between the Skirrid's twin peaks. There's also an odd toadstool-shaped rock on the hillside, known as the Devil's Table, which is where Lucifer was resting before all this commotion occurred. Jack was to further impress the Devil by taking three huge rocks from here and tossing them a distance of 12 miles towards the Wye valley, where they landed in a field near the village of Trelech. There is a small standing stone circle there now and the name Trelech translates as 'town of stones'.

Now you'll probably choose to discount the whole Jack of Kent theory, and instead believe the archaeologists who have dated those stones to Prehistoric times. And you'd be right to, but there's something about these myths and legends which bring a landscape to life, and tales like these make a walk all the more interesting and enjoyable. The mystical tales of the Skirrid certainly have a hold over people's imaginations. Years ago, farmers would take soil from the landslip ravine and sprinkle it on their land to keep bad spirits away and ensure a good harvest.

If you choose to traverse the mountain rather than turn around and go back, you can either take the steep route down the north side or go for the gentle descent offered by the Pilgrim's Path – which was the way worshippers at St Michael's used to take.

The track takes you along the public footpath through farmland and along a back road before emerging alongside Llanvihangel Court. You may hear the peacocks that patrol the grounds here before you see the beautiful Tudor barn which sits alongside the road. Recently restored, it's a listed building and has a spectacular exposed oak timber framework.

Llanvihangel Court is open to the public occasionally, usually in the summer, and is a building with no little history to it – for example, Charles I is alleged to have used it as a refuge during the Civil War.

Having passed the barn you head towards the main road which you have to cross before you see the Skirrid Inn with its famous lightning bolt sign outside the door. It's a great place to grab a spot of lunch or refreshment, and remember they haven't hanged anyone here for years, so you should be quite safe!

The historic Skirrid Inn, Wales's oldest and most haunted pub

Winter

The Blorenge

Near: Blaenavon, Abergavenny

Ordnance Survey Grid Reference SO 254107

OS Explorer Map OL13

Derek says...

The weather on the Blorenge can deteriorate quickly and the terrain is rough and boggy in places but when we did this walk, conditions were almost perfect! We were lucky; we wanted snow and we got it. It was inches deep in places transforming the mountain into a winter wonderland. It was cold but it was crisp and clear, so we could see for miles with fantastic views of the Sugar Loaf mountain, Skirrid and the Brecon Beacons.

This area was once a hive of industrial activity and it's worth stopping to try and imagine what it must have been like in the 1800s when the ironworks were in full swing. These days it's all quiet but tipping can be a problem on the mountain; I stumbled across a burnt-out car. The local authority, however, is working hard to maintain the beauty of the area.

In the winter months you may not see much wildlife but you may see a peregrine falcon or other moorland birds – oh, and lots of sheep!

Finally, have a look around the Blaenavon Ironworks and if you're feeling thirsty pop into the Cordell Country Inn for a glass of shandy!

The trail is an intermediate walk of 12 miles (18k) with two steepish climbs. If this is too much for one day or you want to take in all the points of interest and museums accessible from the trail, the walk is easily split into two loops.

I never tire of taking visitors around this walk. There is always some part that will make them stop and go 'Wow'; be it the spectacular views over the Usk Valley and the Brecon Beacons, a glimpse of a peregrine falcon or a red grouse, the intoxicating scent and sight of a hill full of heather bloom or 'discovering' one of the many archaeological gems. Don't forget, this is the area that inspired Alexander Cordell to write *Rape of the Fair Country*!

The trail is a trip through time, witnessing man's manipulation of the landscape from the bronze-age, through the birth of the industrial revolution and on to the present day. But don't think it is all mines and coal-tips; this is an area rich in natural history and rural traditions. I love to sit by one of the tram-roads, looking down into the valley with only the sound of the wing beats of a jackdaw high above me.

Fiona Ford

Torfaen Borough Council

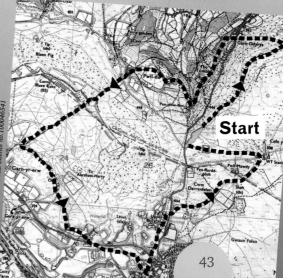

Start

A very cold Keeper's Pond

Walking in winter can often seem a daunting prospect. It's cold (obviously), wet and windy. And if it snows, then the sensible thing to do is to stay at home and crank up the heating until the nights begin to lighten up. Time to enjoy the great indoors rather than the great outdoors – right?

But that's not much fun, is it? Especially when there are some Welsh walks which are actually better in winter than in any other season. And while cold weather, freezing fog and blizzards are to be avoided, sometimes a wander along a snowy mountain path, with blue arctic skies and fresh clean air, is as good as it gets. So if the forecast allows you the chance to get high on a hill on a winter's day, think about heading for Blaenavon and the magnificent Blorenge mountain.

For a start, the area is totally geared up for walkers. The local authority, Torfaen, has steadily built up a network of inter-linking paths of various lengths, aimed at all abilities, each acting to showcase the area's beautiful scenery and rich heritage.

For *Weatherman Walking* we combined parts of the two Iron Mountain Trail paths to give people a flavour of what's on offer. However, you may want to call at the local tourist office before you set out, just to check which paths they would recommend. They produce a pack of walks which are easy to follow and have all the information you need to start reading the landscape and uncovering the story of Blaenavon.

The mountain and town are part of an Industrial Landscape World Heritage Site, which gives them the same protected status as the Taj Mahal and the Great Barrier Reef. It was awarded this special status by the United Nations Educational Science and Cultural Organisation (UNESCO) in November 2000. They singled out the area for attention because Blaenavon was one of the birthplaces of the Industrial Revolution, and because these days no other place in the world has such a collection of buildings, furnaces, casting houses, tunnels, spoil heaps, tramways and machinery left from that time. Blaenavon's unique selling point is that it retains so much of the flotsam and jetsam of industrialisation. And these walks are a great way of seeing the amazing reminders of a long gone and often violent age.

From early attempts at coal mining to vast toxic slag sculptures, from ruined foundries to the coal tips and abandoned tramways, all along these trails you'll find the scars of the area's industrial past. You'll also appreciate how they combine to create a unique Welsh landscape, one with an often bleak but beguiling beauty that will surprise new visitors to the area. If you arrive on a day like the one we filmed on, then you really are in for a treat because a light blanket of snow totally transforms the mountain. It also helps pick out the lumps and bumps, the tram roads and trails that act as clues to the forces that shaped the 'Iron Mountain'.

We started our walk at the car park at Keeper's Pond on the B4246 road between Blaenavon and Abergavenny. The pond appears on some maps as Pen-ffordd-goch Pond, but is known locally as Keeper's Pond, because this was where the local gamekeeper had a cottage. Keeper's Pond is also the sign on the car park, so look for that – not for what's written on the 'proper' map! The pond is man-made and was built to supply water for the forges and works at Garn Ddyrys – an abandoned village that you'll come across later on in the walk.

It also proved useful, however, to the local ironmasters, because this mountain is the furthest south that red grouse naturally occur – so come the glorious 12th, visitors to the Ironworks and Foundry could be offered some grouse shooting as a sweetener to any business they were conducting with the Blaenavon Company. The pond offers some fantastic views of the Sugar Loaf and the Brecon Beacons and there's an information panel that helpfully points out all the mountain peaks. In fact, some visitors are content to just wander around the pond and feed their packed lunch to the sheep – but really you need to be a bit more adventurous to get the best out of the area.

The Iron Mountain Trail is a figure-of-eight walk, with the pond as the centre of its loop – which means you can divide it up into two walks and use Keeper's Pond as your base for both. We cut some corners and did

The crew busy at Blaenavon Ironworks Museum, a unique collection of buildings from Britain's industrial past

half of Walk 1 and most of Walk 2, missing out the Woodland Trust reserve at the Punchbowl, the Cut and Shut tunnel, and the start of the Llanfoist Incline, amongst other points of interest. Instead, we left the pond from the mountainside edge and trekked across the open heath for half a mile before dropping down the side of the mountain to meet up with the flat, straight path provided by the former Hill's Tram Road. Named after one of the Blaenavon ironmasters, Thomas Hill, it was constructed in the 1820s and connected the ironworks with the canal at Llanfoist.

The walk here offers great views of the Skirrid mountain and you'll also pass the Cordell Country Inn, named after the author Alexander Cordell, who chronicled the struggles of the iron workers here with his novel Rape of the Fair Country. It was a best seller when it was published in 1959, and there are now specific walks here which are designed to bring the locations and characters in Cordell's novel to life. By the same token, if you haven't read any of his South Wales sagas, then they're an ideal starting point to get a flavour of what Blaenavon was like 200 years ago at the time of the Industrial Revolution. And in a bizarre twist, the current publisher of Cordell's novels is a company called Blorenge Books!

Reading about the history of this place really pays off as you progress around the mountain, because if you can make the mental contrast between the peace and emptiness you'll encounter here today and the raucous colonisation that existed under the furnace clouds of the old ironworks, then your walk becomes a much more powerful and enlightening experience.

The first real opportunity you have to make these kinds of connections comes when you cross the main road at the end of tram line and stumble into Garn Ddyrys, one of those lost places of the 'Second Iron Age'. It was built in 1817 to process 'pig iron' from the Blaenavon Ironworks to make it a less brittle, more malleable metal. The byproduct of this process was molten slag which was deposited all around Garn Ddyrys and remains there to this day. Not much else of the foundry or the village survives, though, for the simple reason that in the 1860s the company decided to shut down operations there and move them to Blaenavon. The machinery was dismantled and moved to a new site at Forgeside, and the community at Garn Ddyrys – some 300 people in all – were moved along with it. All that is left now is the foundations of a house, the stone arches from the main Forge building and, on the slope to the right of the path, a retaining wall for the upper pond, which supplied water to the steam engines.

One other remnant of its industrial past remains. As you walk away from Garn Ddyrys you'll see a monster-sized lump of slag squatting on the hillside like a dirty brown dinosaur. It's a listed monument and a fascinating reminder of the area's polluted past. It's also something of an iconic local feature – even if it does look like as if it belongs on another planet. The tram road continues around the bend, alongside the ruins of a former blacksmith's forge which also doubled as pub for workers looking for a sneaky pint. Sadly, there are no refreshments available there now, but if you continue on from here you can look down onto the beautiful cwm above the village of Govilon. As you do, think of this view as a glimpse into an older, pre-industrial Blorenge. This is what it might have looked like had it not been scoured and exploited for iron, coal and steel.

The patchwork of fields and farmland here is a real contrast to the barren hills around Blaenavon – so between the two views you have a handy 'before and after' guide to this part of South Wales. From here you ascend the small Rhiw Ifor path, near the Pwll Du Quarry, and pass another man-made reservoir (now drained), known as the Balance Pond. Famous from Cordell's book as the place where the locals went to fight and settle their differences, it was once used to operate a counter-balance lift that raised and lowered trams through a vertical shaft cut into the quarry.

Beyond the pond is the Lamb and Fox pub, almost all that remains of the village of Pwll Du, which was inhabited up until the 1960s. Once a thriving village of over 300 residents which boasted two pubs, two chapels, a school and a shop, it was populated by miners, iron workers, quarrymen and their families. From the 1930s onwards, though, their numbers declined as work dried up, and by 1960 it was declared a slum. The remaining inhabitants were moved out and their houses bulldozed. The old Welfare Hall was also left standing, and these days it's a school's outdoor pursuits centre.

Pwll Du also used to be home to one of the longest tram tunnels in the world: at just over 2km (1¼ miles) long, it was the longest of its kind in Britain. It wound its way for a mile and a half through the mountain to emerge at Garn-yr-erw, and for 50 years horses pulled trams laden with limestone, coal and pig iron through it. These days the tunnels are filled in and the entrances are scheduled monuments. So if you want to continue your tour you have to go over ground. As you do, you'll cross the Canada tips, all that remain of one of Britain's first open cast drift mines. It was based on a Canadian method of mining (hence the name) and started in the 1940s as part of the war effort. And yes, they're a listed monument, too. In fact, this whole mountain is like one massive museum dedicated to telling the story of Wales's industrial heritage – so remember, these tips are just another part of the exhibits! As you climb above them you're in for a real treat as the views on a clear day are stunning.

You can see Pen-y-fan in the Brecon Beacons, as well as getting a terrific view of Coity Mountain and the Big Pit Mining Museum. From here you follow another straight flat track, the Dyne-Steel Incline, which was built in the 1850s by Thomas Dyne-Steel, assistant manager and engineer at Blaenavon Ironworks. The incline replaced the horse-drawn-tram road through the old tunnel, and the steam-driven double incline soon proved a quicker and more cost-effective way of moving goods between Blaenavon and the Monmouthshire and Brecon canal.

At the bottom of the incline you take a sharp left turn and cut across country, past the Hill Pits chimney and onto the main Garn Road (the B4248). This takes you into Blaenavon and alongside the Ironworks Museum. At the time of writing this was closed between October and April, so check ahead if you fancy a look inside. If it is shut, then take five minutes to have a look from the road above at the old workers' cottages, foundry buildings and water tower, as it really is a special place and very evocative.

Following the Iron Mountain trail markers from here, you are taken above the works and alongside a farm wall made of some very strange cylindrical bricks with round holes blown through their ends. These are called Bessemer

Tuyères (pronounced 'tyres'); they were bricks that were built into the base of a Bessemer converter – the device responsible for turning iron into steel. Hot air was blown through them into molten pig iron, removing the impurities and turning them either into gas or a lump of solid slag. As the bricks were thrown away, they were soon reclaimed to make walls and to 'fence off' farmland.

The remnants of an older method of iron production await you as you cross the main road and head towards the twin masts above the 'finishing line' to our walk – Foxhunter's memorial. Here the banks of heather have been eroded by the practice of 'scouring', as well as by other mining activities such as bell pits. Scouring occurred where iron ore lay close to surface of the soil. Small dams were built and small ponds were formed. Once enough water was collected, a sluice gate would be lifted allowing the water to 'scour' away the loose topsoil and expose the ore below.

As you emerge from this rutted landscape, you see the Foxhunter car park, built in the shadow of the famous old horse's grave. Foxhunter is best known for carrying Colonel Sir Harry Llewellyn to Olympic showjumping gold at the Helsinki games in 1952. The team gold was Britain's only gold medal at that games and it helped establish the sport in the imagination of the British public. Foxhunter became the most famous horse in Britain for a time, and when he died in 1959 his heart was buried on the mountain where he had been trained, the impressive rocky gravestone a suitable memorial.

Bessemer Tuyères: bricks that were built into the base of a Bessemer converter

This spot also offers a final set of stunning views that finish the walk off in style. Standing on the grave with the masts to your right, you'll see Monmouthshire sprawled out below you, including the beautiful Usk Valley. And if you turn to your left you'll also see a Bronze Age cairn that stands on the summit point of the Blorenge, about half a mile from the graveside. So it's not just industrial archaeology that they have here – there's a bit of everything.

Half a mile in the opposite direction is the Keeper's Pond, allowing you to arrive back at your starting point. Time it just right and you may get the chance to build a snowman too!

Cwm Idwal, Snowdonia

Near: Bethesda, Capel Curig

Ordnance Survey Grid Reference SH 649604

OS Explorer Map OL17

Derek says...

This walk is easy to get to from the main A5 road. A short walk takes you from the car park up into the mountains. The view down Nant Ffrancon Valley is amazing but come prepared. When I was there in late February we had hail and sleet showers.

Cwm Idwal is a special place and one of the best locations in Britain to see the effects of the last Ice Age. The geological features drew naturalist Charles Darwin here in the 19th century. Botanists still come to study the rare arctic-alpine plants such as the Snowdon Lily which is under threat from global warming.

I love all the area's Welsh names: Clogwyn y Geifr (the cliff of the goats), Pen yr Ole Wen (top of the white light) and Twll Du (black hole, but known in English as the Devil's Kitchen). A plume of cloud can rise like steam from the Devil's Kitchen; when viewed by ships at sea it was thought to be an omen. It is however simply caused by moist air hitting the rock face, forcing it upwards, so that it cools and condenses, forming swirling clouds.

The sight of Llyn Idwal is breathtaking, nestling as it does in the north, facing Cwm Idwal, and surrounded by the high peaks of Y Garn and Y Glyder Fawr. It is rare to find so many glaciation features in such a small area: moraines, rock striations, roche moutonnees, erratic boulders and exposed rock strata in the high cliffs. Arctic-alpine plants also abound: if you're lucky you may come across the small and fragile *Lloydia serotina,* the Snowdon Lily. Seek out the right type of rock and you never know what plants you might find.

It is reputed that no bird flies over the lake, because of a terrible accident in the past. It is said that the carer of young Prince Idwal neglected his duties, allowing him to fall to his death from the cliffs of Twll Du.

Hywel Roberts
Snowdonia National Park

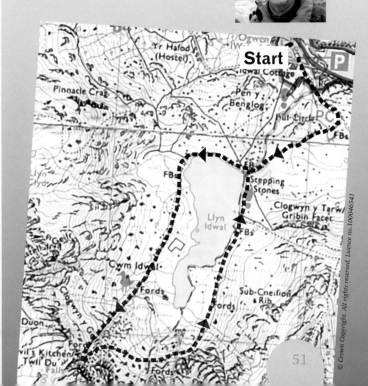

51

Cwm Idwal was the first walk that we ever did on *Weatherman Walking* – way back in 2003 when it was a new show for Radio Wales, and a television programme was beyond the realms of possibility!

We chose it then because it offered so much for so many different types of walkers. Beginners and novices could take the path as far as the lake and still get a feel of this incredible landscape, while more accomplished walkers could head up towards the Devil's Kitchen and to the very top of the mountain – a route that delivers stunning views but which needs to be negotiated with a certain amount of hiking savvy!

It's a well-marked path; there's a car park right off the A5 main road, and there's a tea bar and a youth hostel too, so all kinds of visitors are catered for. More importantly, it's one of the most easily readable examples of a glaciated landscape in Wales and is jaw-droppingly beautiful whatever the season or weather. The only drawback here is that it can be a very busy path, particularly on weekends. You're also likely to see lots of school parties being dragged around by enthusiastic Geography teachers – so watch out for lots of sulky teenagers in kagouls!

Even when it's busy, though, you can still get some peace and quiet and the shores of the lake offer walkers a great opportunity to sit back, take a break, search for fossils or to try and spot the wild Welsh mountain goats that graze on the slopes above.

The walk breaks down into two options, one more ambitious than the other. The first, easy part of the route takes you along a well-laid stone step path up to and around the lake. It's well marked and there's a map at the Visitor Centre if you want to check it out beforehand. The second option allows you to climb up the mountain above the lake, past the Idwal Slabs towards the Devil's Kitchen and back down. There are longer routes, some of which take you up onto the ridge above the lake, along Glyder Fawr and Glyder Fach, which give stunning views of the area. But be warned: we've been here three times now to record and research the location and have never made it further than fifty feet from the top – bad weather has forced us back on every occasion! So if you do fancy the more demanding paths,

The stone path that takes you all the way up to the lake

then bear in mind that they have some challenging sections which in poor visibility can be very difficult. Good map and compass skills are essential here, but if the weather allows you an opportunity to get up on top, then the views will more than reward your effort.

For less adventurous walkers, this is what we suggest: from the car park you follow the path to an ornate iron gate. It was designed by one of the seasonal wardens as a tribute to Evan Roberts, who was the first ever warden of Cwm Idwal back in 1953. Evan Roberts was a champion of the special arctic alpines and rare plants that are found in the area, and his encyclopaedic knowledge of the terrain and its plant life was legendary – in fact, there's also a painting of him at the visitor centre.

The gate is worth a second look as it's sculpted to resemble the climb ahead. The top part reflects the topography around Twll Du, while the rails reflect the geology of the area and the reflection of the moraines in the lake – Llyn Idwal.

The gate opens on to a magical wooden bridge that spans a fantastic waterfall, and looks for all the world like a scene from Tolkien's *Lord of the Rings*. It's a great early selling point for the walk, as most routes don't have anything this beautiful at the end of a trek – let alone at the start! As soon as you cross the bridge, the path climbs steadily upwards and each bend reveals great views of the surrounding mountains such as Y Garn and Pen yr Ole Wen, which in English translates as the 'Top of the White Light'.

As you head up the path, remember that 100 years ago – when the land was part of the Penrhyn estate – this was a coach route, with poor horses having to negotiate the climb. Then the route was used mainly by fishermen heading for the lake, and at times you can spot the remains of an old sunken rowing boat.

More obvious are the signs of glacial erosion. On the right of the path is an enormous 'erratic boulder'. This is a rock that was picked up in another part of the country by the ice flow and then deposited miles from its original source as the ice melted. You can tell what actually happened because it's a different rock type to that found in its final resting place.

Hywel and Derek disappearing into the distance with Llyn Idwal behind them

Some of the new heather growing back on the mountain since the suspension of grazing

Above the boulder you begin to get a good view of the classic hanging valley that surrounds the lake and the fearsome steep rise of the Twll Du, which means 'Black Hole' – the original name for the Devil's Kitchen.

The lake itself is 800 metres long and 300 metres wide and feeds the Idwal stream that babbles down alongside the main path. Stand on the bridge over the stream at the base of the lake and gaze up at the vast bowl above. It was literally scraped out by a glacier thousands of years ago, and near the base of the slopes you can see the rock and debris left by the ice as it moved downward. The mounds on the northern shore are called moraines, and are another sign of glaciation. Legend had it that these were the burial mounds of Prince Idwal and his men – actually, they are just mounds of rock fragments and clay 'bulldozed' into place by the glaciers some time between 13,000 and 11,500 years ago.

While we're on the subject of glaciation, there are two more things worth talking about – although to see them you'll have to take a slight detour from the main path. If you turn right at the lake and head for the brow of the hill, you'll see a huge rocky outcrop – one side smooth and the other ripped and scarred. These are known as roches moutonnées. They are one of the more visible signs of glacial erosion and demonstrate two ways in which a glacier can erode the surface of the rock. At the base of a glacier, large amounts of rock and sediment are incorporated into the ice. As the glacier moves along, these held fragments begin to act like the teeth of a large file, sliding over the rock and scouring it smooth – it's a feature known as glacial abrasion and glacial polish. This is what causes the smooth head of the roche moutonnée. The other method of erosion in evidence here is called 'plucking'. This is where the ice has frozen into cracks in the rock and, as the glacier moves, that ice is pulled back, tearing away at the rock as it does so. The intensity of the plucking is greatest on the lee-side of rock mounds. So roches moutonnées are smooth on the side of ice advancement and steep and jagged on the opposite side. This is what gives them their bizarre asymmetrical appearance, which some say looks like a sheep's head – hence the name.

Directly in front of those rocks is a spectacular view of the Nant Ffrancon valley, a huge U-shaped valley with the river Ogwen snaking through it. On a clear day you can look out from here out to the Irish Sea, and it was the view from the opposite direction that led to this spot being called the 'Devil's Kitchen'. Sailors staring out on the landscape saw the mist swirling around the Twll Du, and to them it seemed as if a great big boiling cloud of steam was constantly rising from the cleft cut between the rocks at the centre of the bowl. The reason behind the phenomenon has less to do with the supernatural and more to do with the weather. Wind blows in from the sea and rushes up against the sheer cliff walls of the Cauldron; it then cools and forces the warm air up, thereby creating that steaming cloud along the way.

As you walk back towards the main path, take a look up at Tryfan. Fix your gaze on the profile of the top ridge and ask yourself – who does that profile remind me of? Some suggestions have been a Neolithic cave man, a Native American Indian Chief in a head-dress, and even Homer Simpson! Most people though think it looks like Queen Victoria – lying down and definitely not amused!

The Twll Du

Returning to the main path and heading around the lake, you'll find yourself on the pebble 'beach' of the lake. It's a good place to stop and catch your breath, and while you're there you can watch to see if any birds fly across the surface of the water. Why? Well, legend has it that during the 12th century, Owain, Prince of Gwynedd, decided to entrust the care of his son Idwal to a man called Nefydd Hardd. Nefydd was envious of Idwal, who was good-looking and very clever. His own son Dunawd wasn't the prettiest or the brightest and had precious little talent to speak of in any department. Whether it was the envious father or the useless son, we'll never know, but somebody decided that Idwal needed a permanent vacation and pushed him down the slopes into the lake, where he drowned.

After his son died, Owain banished Nefydd from his kingdom and named the lake Llyn Idwal, in memory of his son. Since that day no bird has flown over the lake's surface, and legend also has it that a wailing voice can be heard whenever there is a storm in the Cwm.

However, if the idea of bird watching doesn't appeal to you, then check out the stones beneath your feet for fossils. Millions of years ago, this land was under the sea and fossilised seashells and creatures are fairly easy to find if you're prepared to scrabble around in the stones and gravel.

Leaving the beach, the path begins to climb and the landscape starts to change. Thirty years ago, the Park began fencing off parts of the land – to control erosion from walkers and to see what would happen if the sheep on the mountain weren't allowed to graze. Over the years, these schemes have been extended, and now you can appreciate the difference as heather, wild flowers and even trees have begun to grow on the slopes. Currently there is an agreement between the National Trust, the Snowdonia National Park Authority and the Countryside Council for Wales that there should be no grazing allowed in the valley because of these long-term vegetation studies. However, you'll still see small herds of Welsh mountain goats on the hills. So far, they've escaped the ban and at least walkers get the chance to catch these magnificent animals in the wild.

As you follow the path under the Twll Du you'll see the more advanced route snaking up the mountainside. That will take you to the bottom of the black cleft and then on up onto the ridge. Less adventurous souls can keep walking across the mountain, although there is a tricky crossing at a waterfall which you need to be careful about. If you were to choose the higher route then you'll be rewarded with the discovery of a few hidden treasures, although they are small and to an untrained eye not particularly interesting. However, to many they are the most important feature of the Park.

Cwm Idwal is often talked of as 'Nature's Hanging Garden' – a title earned for the amazing number of rare and colourful arctic alpine plants that cling to its steep slopes. It's long been a Mecca for botanists and naturalists, from Victorian plant collectors to scientists such as Charles Darwin. And while on the surface it looks like any other part of the Snowdonia landscape, a close look in the boulder scree and the rock faces reveals small clumps of colourful plants. These plants are species that grow in the Arctic or at high altitudes in mountainous areas. They need cold conditions and freedom from competition from more aggressive species which grow in less extreme environments. And while they are relatively small in number compared to places such as the Alps, or the mountains of Scandinavia or the Scottish Highlands, they are arguably more significant. As this is the furthest south these species appear in Europe at such a low altitude, they are closely monitored, because if global warming kicks in then these would be some of the first plants to disappear. In effect, these plants act like a barometer for global warming and are therefore internationally important.

So if you do make it up here, try and spot the moss campion, the purple, mossy and starry saxifrages, the pretty white Snowdon lily, and the insectivorous butterwort which catches insects in its leaves before devouring them. They are joined by plants normally found in woodlands – angelica, wood anemones, and roseroot, the toothache plant. You'll also see devil's bit scabious, and even thrift – which is usually found on the coast. Collectively, they all combine to add colour to the grey cliff walls although excepting the purple saxifrage (which can flower in February) you'll have to come here in summer to appreciate the 'hanging gardens' in their full glory.

Back on our 'main route', the path continues over the waterfall and soon starts to head down. As it does so, look up on your right hand side and you'll see the famous Idwal Slabs – a fairly smooth, vertical rock face that's a popular destination for climbers. The original Welsh name for the Slabs is 'Rhiwiau Caws'. It probably hasn't caught on with the climbers as it translates as 'Slopes of Cheese' – which doesn't sound quite like the kind of rock face a mountain man or woman should be boasting about climbing! Once you're past the Slabs you hit the lakeside path once again, and from there it's an easy walk back down to the visitor centre and car park.

Before you go, promise yourself that you'll come back and try the walk again in a different season, because it's only by returning – when the snow is off the high slopes and the flowers start to change the colour of the Cwm – that you'll appreciate the real evolving beauty of the place.

Kenfig Dunes

Near: Porthcawl

Ordnance Survey Grid Reference SS 802809

OS Explorer Map 151

Derek says...

South Wales is blessed with some lovely beaches and although I've lived here for most of my life, I didn't realise this wonderful nature reserve was right on my doorstep. Finding such hidden locations is one of the treats of working on the *Weatherman Walking* series. Kenfig is really worth making a detour for and is suitable for dog walkers, joggers and horse riders as well as ramblers. It's a great walk to do in winter, especially on a fine and crisp day.

There are plenty of plants and birdlife to spot. Walking on the dunes can be hard going at times, but the path here is quite gentle and the grass cover here means that even with strong, gusty winds you won't get covered in sand!

Each twist and turn on the route reveals something different in the landscape, but my favourite part is when you arrive at Sker Beach.

On a clear day you can see for miles across the Bristol Channel. You also get a good view of Swansea, the Gower Peninsula and the Port Talbot steel works as well!

Kenfig National Nature Reserve isone of the last remnants of a huge sand dune system that once stretched along the coast of South Wales from the River Ogmore to the Gower peninsula.

Kenfig, now a Special Area of Conservation, was once a thriving town. In late medieval times huge storms took their toll and the town was engulfed beneath thousands of tons of sand. The only trace left today of the ancient Borough is the castle keep which rises out of the northern sand. For the last 700 years, nature has colonised the sand and the area is now home to thousands of species of plants and animals including the rare Fen Orchid for which the site is internationally famous.

The land is owned by trustees – successors to the burgesses of the medieval Borough – but is managed by Bridgend County Borough Council. Without management, the dunes would be overcome by dense grassland and scrub woodland which would mean the loss of much of the wildlife of Kenfig.

Graham Holmes
Kenfig National Nature Reserve

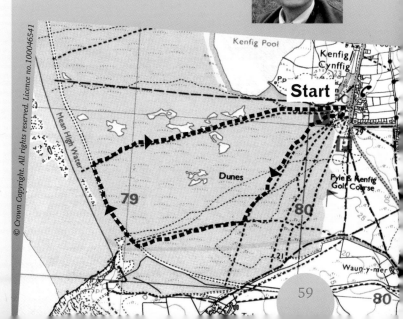

They may look like very different places, but all our Winter walks share a common theme or two – they are all set in landscapes which are still undergoing environmental change, and are all areas which have been sculpted, to varying extents, by man. In the case of our final winter walk, it's the last stronghold of a huge dune system that once stretched along the coast of South Wales from the river Ogmore to the Gower peninsula.

Close to the popular holiday resort of Porthcawl, and bordered by the sprawl of the local steelworks, Kenfig is one of Britain's most important sites for nature conservation. But not only is it an environment that has had to be protected from human exploitation, it's also a place that nature has constantly recreated, sometimes with devastating effect. At least it was devastating for the ancient town of Kenfig, which gave up its battle against the shifting sands more than 700 years ago. And if you think you'll only find tales of towns disappearing under sandstorms in the exotic Middle East, then maybe you should make a trip to Kenfig Dunes. It's a place you can visit at any time of year, and even though the walk steers you past a wild stormy Atlantic beach front, it's a path you can feel confident about taking, even on the coldest of days. It's also a walk that delivers sightings of some wildlife too.

In 1953, Kenfig Dunes were one the first three sites in Wales to be awarded Site of Special Scientific Interest status. It was, however, a court case in the 1960s that created the conditions which have led to this area becoming one of the foremost nature reserves in South Wales.

The case sprang up out of a dispute over ownership. Businessmen representing the Margam estates laid claim to the land, but the local people protested they had a right of ownership which went back as far as the Middle Ages. The case went to the High Court and the locals had to pledge their homes and life savings to the cause just to have their case heard. Thankfully, the judge found in their favour – if he hadn't, the dunes would have been subjected to commercial development and the unique ecosystem here would have been lost. The victorious residents applied to the local authority to make the area a nature reserve, and in 1978 their

wish was granted. A warden was appointed, and finally the dunes were properly managed and protected. In 1989 they were further protected when the beach area became a National Nature Reserve, and in 2005 it was listed as a Special Area of Conservation – which meant that its importance was recognised on a European scale.

So what makes this place so special? Well, the main reason is that the 1,300-acre site provides a wonderful mosaic of environments and habitats. For example, the system has a number of dune slacks – seasonally flooded hollows that provide a home for the reserve's rarest plant, the fen orchid. In fact, 95% of the national fen orchid population can be found here. The area also boasts Kenfig Pool, a 70-acre freshwater pool which is the largest body of fresh water in Glamorgan and home to a host of bird life. The Dunes are a popular destination for bird watchers and plant lovers, but everyone who visits the site should be aware that this is a precious landscape which is constantly evolving all around you. Back in the 1950s, the dunes were made up of 45% bare sand; nowadays it's around 2%. Those sand dunes, which support very rare and specialised plants, are becoming colonised and changed by more aggressive and hardier types of vegetation. The walk actually takes you from these rather overgrown areas down to the more sandy dunes, and you can see the landscape changing as you wander through the three miles of track. As such, it's a short walk but a rewarding and interesting one – and it's always good to get some sand on your shoes in the winter!

It's easy enough to find. From the M4 you follow signs for Porthcawl and North Cornelly and from there you'll find signs that will steer you towards the Nature Reserve. From the car park, the official circular route takes you through the dry dune system, which is accessible all year round. It's also a very well-signed path, with wooden markers popping up every hundred yards or so to keep you on track. But as you follow the markers, keep an eye on the ground that changes beneath your feet. Forty years ago those changes were partly influenced by man, as sand and gravel was extracted from here for industrial purposes. These days, though, the changes to the dunes are all natural. The sand is slowly disappearing due to a process called ecological succession, whereby conditions created by plant colonisation naturally lead to a change in the environment. There are five different stages to the overall change affecting Kenfig – that is, from bare sand to early forest – and each of those stages can be seen here. That final stage would see the creation of an oak forest, but that will take some time to be fully realised – about 150 years, in fact! And when you bear in mind that the last time this area was covered by an oak forest was 4,000 years ago you can appreciate the gradual but constant ecological pressure the landscape is under.

The beginning of the path is covered with bracken and bramble, and it is this section which has changed most significantly from the original dune system. In summer you'll see white throats and willow warblers here, as well as the reserve's rarest bird, the Cetti's warbler. Winter, though, is often the best time for birds here, as the weather regularly blows migrating birds off course, sending them here where they can land, rest and feed. It's also the time of year to see bitterns near the pool and they start arriving here from October onwards, leaving between March and April. And as for the raptors – buzzards, kestrels and marsh harriers also frequent this part of the walk. In fact, when we were recording here, we watched a buzzard, perched on top of one of the dunes, for close to five minutes, while all the time we speculated about what animal it had its eye on in the undergrowth below!

About half a mile along, the path begins to deliver the kind of undulating walk the dunes are famous for. It's never too strenuous, though, and by walking here you may do the environment some good. The weight of human traffic often breaks up the vegetation on the path, allowing the wind to work away at the ground and free up new sandy areas. It pays to look down at your feet here too. That way you'll see some of the plants that make this place so special. On the sandier parts of the path you may see a small flower with soft pale purple, heart-shaped petals. This is rest harrow, so called because as a dry soil plant it has an extensive, stringy root system. And in the days of the horse-drawn plough those long tangled roots proved too tough for the blade to cut through, halting the ploughing – hence the name. In summer, these areas have a tastier treat at your feet – the delicious dewberries that grow here. In fact, come here in August and you'll see walkers returning with plastic containers full of them!

Other plants that might catch your eye on this first mile of the walk are the flea bane (apparently so-named because when it is burned it keeps the flies away) and rose bay willow herb. It's also known as fireweed because, during World War II, it was the first plant to flourish in bomb craters, thriving on the phosphorous deposits that were left in the soil by the explosives.

Kenfig Castle

The closer you get to the seashore, the more prominent the dunes are, and the less thick the vegetation. It's at this part of the trail that the path takes you to Sker Point, which marks the beginning of the Nature Reserve. The beach extends northwards from here for about 7 miles and the reserve ends where the river Kenfig reaches the sea. One more plant to look out for here – and one with a winter theme – is sea holly. It's actually a member of the carrot family, but it looks like holly and is found near the sea, so the name sounds fairly accurate! It's paler than holly, with a blue-green tinge, although it's just as sharp to the touch.

The beach itself is popular with fishermen and has a long mussel bed which can be seen when the tide is out. It also has an impressive shingle ridge created by the tide which, in the absence of any sand to deposit, moves the rock around with awesome ease. If the weather and tide allow it, you may want to take advantage of the long flat beach and get some sand on the soles of your shoes. If not, you can stick to the old haulage road that runs parallel to it and which has been incorporated into the path. It was originally built in the 1960s to take limestone from the South Cornelly quarry to build a deep water harbour in the nearby steelworks. As you walk up this path you'll get a clear view of the steelworks, which was built back in the 1950s on a former wetland site. It's a real contrast to the rich natural environment of Kenfig and a glimpse of what might have happened had the dunes' importance not been recognised and protected.

Leaving the old road you head back on the dune path and rise above the dune system. From this elevated view you can see an orange-coloured house in the distance on your right. This is Sker House, a former grange used and farmed by monks from Neath Abbey. After the dissolution it

went into private ownership and over the years fell into disrepair. It was compulsorily purchased by Bridgend Council in 1996 and then sold to the Buildings At Risk Trust which renovated it and restored it to its former glory. Today it's back in private ownership, although there are occasional guided visits held throughout the year.

As the path heads towards the pool, there are two sections worth pointing out. The first is one of those Dune Slacks, which the wardens usually clear to keep the habitat safe for those rare fen orchids. In this case, though, they've allowed other plants to colonise the area, letting the hollow generate towards another stage of Ecological Succession. This one occupies a stage where mosses, creeping willows and grey willows have established themselves in the wet environment. In time the dead leaves will collect and gradually help turn the clay ground into healthier soil. This in turn will encourage different plants to take over the area, propelling the former wetland site into another stage of Ecological Succession.

Immediately following this hive of plant activity is a sandy hollow known as a 'Blow Out'. The big mound borders the path like a giant inverted sandy cone, with a middle initially scooped out by explosions over 60 years ago. Back in the 1940s the dunes were closed to the public and housed a group of American infantry who used Kenfig as a training ground for the Normandy Landings. They built bridges across the dunes and used the beach for target practice. The hollow is one of those former targets and was the subject of a sustained battering from small arms and mortar fire. Over the years children have claimed the hollow as a playground and kept it clear of vegetation, allowing the wind to maintain it as a small 'blow out'. If you're feeling adventurous, climb inside the big natural sandpit and take in the view of the pool in the distance.

From the blow hole it's a five-minute walk to the shores of this big blue oasis. It's a beautiful clear expanse of water bordered by reed beds with two purpose-built bird-watching hides. There is an access path right the way around the pool and you'll see great crested grebes, gulls, wild fowl and a host of smaller birds as well as those famous bitterns. It's also home to the

Reserve's rarest creature, the medicinal leech, which is so scarce that it has been placed on the Red Data Book List, the list which logs the most endangered species in the country. But you're not very likely to run into one on your walk (unless you've seriously taken the wrong route!).

From the pool, it's a short walk back to the car park, although the Dunes have one more treasure which may tempt you further afield. There are legends that the remains of a medieval village lie beneath these shifting sands. It's not strictly true, but at the edge of the reserve are the remains of Kenfig castle. Established by the Norman invader Robert Fitzhamon, Earl of Gloucester, in the first half of the 12th century, the castle was originally made of wood and was continually attacked by the local Welsh lords, as well as the great Llywelyn and, later still, Owain Glyndŵr. Replaced with a stone castle, gradually a town called Kenfig grew up around it, with a thousand inhabitants drawn by the trade from the river. Unfortunately for the fledgling community, they may have survived guerrilla attacks from the Welsh princes but they couldn't withstand the sustained attack of the elements.

The weather pattern that created this once huge dune system began here in earnest in the 1200s. For 200 years sandstorms battered the settlement, making life intolerable. The last families moved out in the 1400s and all that remains now is the keep of the old castle, still visible above the sand. If you want to investigate it, head for the nearby Angel pub when you get to the end of this route and walk down to the remains from there. It should take you about 15 minutes to get there, and although the castle isn't too impressive these days, remember that in its heyday it was a significant structure and probably stretched to nearly 60 feet in height.

As you get above the pool and head on the last 50 yards to home ground, you'll notice that the path has been covered with tarmac. This is part of a project to make the dunes accessible for disabled visitors, providing a level walkway all the way from the car park to a special viewing platform above the wetlands. It means that even on a stormy, cold winter's day, everyone can have a taste of this wild Atlantic coastline and appreciate an environment rich in wildlife but also one which is constantly changing before your eyes.

Part of the blow hole created by the military training back in the 40s

Spring

St David's Peninsula

Near: St David's
Ordnance Survey Grid Reference SM 740242
OS Explorer Map OL35

Derek says...

This part of Pembrokeshire is one of the sunniest in Wales, with over 1800 hours of sunshine on average a year but as the coast is exposed, it can be windy at times. However, the cliffs around St Justinian's are sheltered from the worst of the wind by Ramsey Island. This encourages an array of flowers in spring, while the cliffs and waters also provide a variety of animal, bird and marine life. While I was there I was lucky to see a few seals and even the odd porpoise!

I was amazed by the extreme force of the tides in Ramsey Sound and the Bitches rapids. This is due to the meeting of the waters of the Irish Sea and St George's Channel.

Both Porth Clais harbour and Whitesands Bay are stunning. The latter is a great place for surfers and there's a nice café here too.

The plus point of this walk is that you can leave your car at the visitor centre in St David's and then catch a bus to be dropped off along the route. If you get tired, just wait by the roadside and they'll come and pick you up.

Why choose Porth Clais to Traeth Mawr (Whitesands)? Well, this is world-class walking by any standards – particularly if the wildlife turn up: porpoise, seals, sea birds galore, ravens, maybe even sun fish. The flowers are more reliable, though!

April and May are best. It is so special that the whole walk is a Site of Special Scientific Interest, though you don't need to be a scientist to see that this place deserves special care. As to the wild majesty of this fantastic coastline, well I can offer a money-back guarantee. So come rain, shine, gale or fog (probably the lot if you take the whole day) this is one walk that should linger long in the memory. The growing problem around St David's during the holiday periods is of car parking and congestion, so please help by minimizing your car use – try the buses, or better still, cycle or walk wherever you can.

Ian Meopham
Pembrokeshire Coast National Park

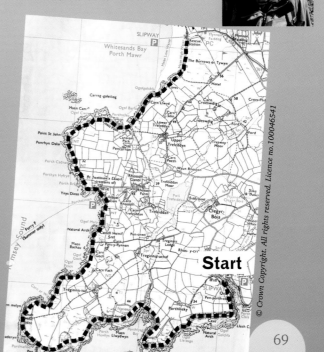

Start

69

The Pembrokeshire Coastal Path is a 186 mile long route around some of the most beguiling parts of West Wales. It's Britain's only true coastal National Park, and even though it attracts hundreds of thousands of visitors every year you are guaranteed to find a corner somewhere that allows you to avoid the crowds and find some peace and quiet.

Porth Clais harbour

The park contains one of the largest densities of protected environment sites in Europe and has an unbeatable selection of stunning scenery – from rugged cliffs to beautiful beaches, woodland estuaries and mysterious islands. It's also a year-round attraction, with each season revealing something new – so it pays to make repeated visits here. If you arrive in Autumn, for instance, you'll be treated to the sight of hundreds of seal cubs being raised on the path's more protected bays and inlets.

Boats near St Justinian's

In Spring though, the area is just starting to burst into bloom, with the slopes and fields carpeted with a colourful blanket of flowers, from the yellow kidney vetch to purple-headed thrift. Not only that, but parts of the walk are scented with a coconut-like fragrance from the rows and rows of gorse bushes that throw a golden cordon around the path. And while it's not exactly a yellow brick road that you follow, the bushes do give the place a sunshine glow – whatever the weather.

Spring is also a great time of the year to go bird watching here, with the nesting sea birds returning to the cliffs to breed and feed. And if it's the more exotic types of wildlife you're after, you'll also see pods of dolphins and porpoises, along with the seals, in the waters around Ramsey Island. And if they don't show, then don't worry – you'll always see the ponies that graze the gorse-covered hills. All in all, it adds up to a walk with lots of colour, wildlife, life-affirming views and clean fresh air. Not only that, but the sunny Pembrokeshire weather means you can still get lucky and come back from your walk with a tan.

We walked from the pretty little harbour of Porth Glais to the popular beach of Whitesands, taking in views of Ramsey Island and the lifeboat station at St Justinian's. Our starting point, however, was the city of St David's itself. It's about a mile and a half from Porth Glais but, thanks

Two views of the treacherous Bitches

to a walker-friendly bus service, it's the ideal place to start exploring the coastal path. St David's may be Britain's smallest city, with a population of just 2,000 lucky residents, but tourists swell those modest numbers beyond all recognition during the summer months. So to cope with the human traffic – and to get the accompanying cars off the road – there is a network of buses that can drop walkers off all over the surrounding area. It means you can leave your car behind and let someone else navigate the narrow lanes. Not only that, but if you get tired on your walk just head back to the main road and hail the next bus you see.

A five-minute bus ride will get you as far as the National Trust car park at Porth Glais. You then head for the sea, past the old lime kilns, along the harbour.

The path is easy to follow from start to finish – just remember to keep the sea on your left at all times and you'll be fine! The harbour supports a couple of fishing boats that go potting for crabs and lobster from here, and it's also a base for various outdoor pursuits such as sea kayaking and coasteering.

A winding path takes you up through some blackthorn bushes (which should be covered in white blossom at this time of year) and onto the yellow gorse-coloured cliff tops. Immediately below you, to your left, on the other side of the harbour are the rocks of Trwyn Cynddeiriog or 'Furious Point' – aptly named when you see the waves come crashing in to this distinctive headland.

Just above the path is a beautifully restored traditional Pembrokeshire cottage, painted in white and blue with a tell-tale 'concrete roof'. Local slate quarried at Abereiddi is quite porous and brittle and would start to leak after a few years' use. So, to increase the life of their roofs, people would coat the slate with a cement wash. Successive washes, however, added to the weight of the roof, causing it to avalanche off. Undeterred, people began to cement strips of barbed wire into the structure, hooking the ends under the eaves to hold the whole lot together. If you look closely you will see ridges and creases, caused by the wire, running down the sides of the roof. Obviously, building methods have changed in Pembrokeshire over the years so the 'barbed wire look' is harder to find, but you will spot one or two as you walk around St David's.

As you head down the main path through the gorse, you'll probably catch sight of the ponies on the hills around you. They belong to the National Trust and are part of a strategy aimed at keeping the bushes under control. The Trust also graze cattle on the slopes and have a programme of gorse burning for some sections of the walk – but the horses are the most popular method of control as far as the tourists are concerned. One word of caution, though – please don't feed them. It encourages the horses to come looking for food from ramblers and not everyone appreciates the attention.

The other word of caution is that if you're not a fan of dizzying drops, then do keep away from the edge of the path; at certain points the cliffs fall away quite steeply and sharply. Also, as parts of the cliff face regularly collapse, these drops can crop up all the way along the route, so always follow signs for diversions. This isn't a particularly dangerous path, far from it, but you do have to be cautious. Think of it in the same way as the walk you take alongside a busy road. If you stick to the pavement you're safe,

Despite all appearance to the contrary these men are not trapped by a wall of gorse – there is a path through these bushes and guide Ian Meopham is trying to get our weatherman safely through it

The lifeboat station at St Justinian's

but if you step onto the road you're asking for trouble. And while part of the attraction here is the thrill of walking close to this wild, rugged coastline, it pays to be sensible when you're out on the cliffs.

Speaking of dangerous stretches of coastline, the great selling point for this walk is that it takes you past Ramsey Sound, with spectacular views of Ramsey Island and the infamous group of rocks known as the Bitches. The tide rips through here with a ferocious power, churning the water around the Island. It also changes direction daily, heading north for 6 hours before reversing south again. It was on the Bitches that the community of St David's lost the *Gem* lifeboat back in 1910. The 12-oared sailing lifeboat had been in service since 1825, but went down with the loss of three crewmen after being wrecked on rocks in the boiling waters of Ramsey Sound. The *Gem* had been called out in a storm to rescue the crew of the *Democrat*, a ketch that had been trying to shelter from the weather near Ramsey Island. The *Gem* rescued all three members of the boat before hitting the rocks and going down itself. The survivors swam to the Bitches and climbed onto the rocks where they waited to be picked up.

This treacherous stretch of water also boasts several other dangerous rocks and reefs, including the Bishops and the Clerks. But while it may be a hazard to boats, it's a haven for marine life because of the nutrient-rich waters. It's here that you'll best spot the porpoises, known locally by the fishermen as 'puffing pigs' because of the snuffling sounds they make as they break the surface to breathe.

If you're lucky, you'll also see the amazing aerial display of the gannets dive-bombing into the ocean to stab at the fish, their wings folding back as they angle their descent into the water. It's also a good spot for cormorants and shags although one of the more unique species to nest here on the cliffs isn't a sea bird at all. They are the chough, one of Britain's rarest birds and a member of the crow family. In fact they look very similar to crows, the only difference being their red beaks and red legs.

It's not just wildlife that makes this walk special. It wouldn't be a Welsh walk without some sign of an industrial heritage, and here it's copper mining that provides the link with the past. There was a fledgling copper mining industry here in the early 19th century, although it was never on the scale of similar enterprises in Cornwall and was obviously nowhere near as successful – much to the benefit of the local environment. You'll encounter the remains of two mines on this walk, Treginis Copper Mine, which was worked between 1820 and 1836, and Porth Taflod mine, which operated around forty years later.

Porth Taflod has a tragic history and was closed after a practical joke went fatally wrong. The men who worked the seam were lowered up and down the shaft by means of a large metal bucket that could only carry one worker at a time. On May 2nd 1883, two of the men on the surface tried to play a trick on a fellow worker called John Reynolds, who was being lifted up from the tunnel below. They stopped the winch as the bucket was rising, in an attempt to shake it and scare their workmate. Unfortunately for all concerned, the bucket flipped back, tipping the hapless miner out and breaking his neck in the ensuing fall. He died a few days later and the two would-be pranksters were tried for manslaughter. They were acquitted and the mine was closed soon after. All that remains of it today are some stone ruins and an old shaft, which is fenced off for obvious reasons.

As the path bends around the coastline there are a few landmarks that let you know that you're heading in the right direction. The solitary mountain of Carn Llidi, which rises above Whitesands Beach, is a constant reminder that you're on the right track, while the iconic lifeboat station at St Justinian's is another. The red and white boathouse is due to be replaced, but it's been a familiar part of the coastline here since 1911.

St Justinian, who gives his name to this cove, was a contemporary of Saint David, although a much more hardcore kind of Christian. He felt that life with the monks on the mainland was far too easy-going, and instead struck out for Ramsey where he founded a more hard-line colony. Unfortunately for him, it proved a little too tough for his followers who, chaffing under the strain of his authoritarian leadership and the Spartan lifestyle, rebelled, attacking their spiritual leader and beheading him. Legend has it, though, that this violent act did little to stop Justinian, who simply picked up his head, stuck it under his arm and left them on the island, hacking away at the rocky path to the mainland as he went. The result of his sword swinging was the Bitches, which continue to this day to wag a stern and forbidding finger at anyone who dares trifle with them.

Passing the lifeboat house you'll see the remains of a medieval church dedicated to Justinian. The ruins are on private ground, but can be seen quite easily from the path as you hit the final stretch of the walk before Whitesands. There is still plenty of wildlife and plant life to watch out for here. You may see the St Mark's fly, which emerges at this time of year (allegedly around April 25th, St Mark's day, hence the name) and congregates on the gorse bushes. They may be an irritant as they swarm and buzz around, but remember they only live for two or three days so they're not the kind of pest which will hang around all spring.

You'll pass the bays and caves here that are so popular with the seals in autumn, and as for spring flowers, you'll see lots of white sea campion, yellow kidney vetch, and thrift. You might also spot some scurvy grass, so called because sailors used to eat it as a source of vitamin C – vital if you wanted to avoid the old sea dog's disease. If you're tempted to try it, you'll soon realise what an awful experience scurvy was – it had to be, because there's no other reason why you would willingly chew on this sour-tasting plant!

As the path gets sandier you'll start to glimpse the beach at Whitesands – or Porth Mawr, as it's called in Welsh. It's a beautiful beach, one of the best in Pembrokeshire, and a big favourite of surfers – you'll no doubt see plenty of them riding the waves near the Ram's Head rock. It's also popular with kayakers, divers, windsurfers and anglers, and the large west-facing expanse of sand can become very crowded in the summer months when tourists flock to the area. In Spring, however, you might get lucky and find that you have the place all to yourself, although be warned – there's a ban on dogs using the sands, which runs from May 1st to September 30th. So if you take your pet with you while walking, then you may have to miss the beach and stay on the path.

Whitesands Beach

The beach has played an important part in the commerce and life of Pembrokeshire for some time and was a meeting-point from as far back as the Bronze Age for people using the land and sea routes to Ireland. In fact, there are traces of a 6th century chapel dedicated to St Patrick, buried beneath the dunes behind the beach. Whitesands makes for a great end to the walk. There are shops and a restaurant here, all based at the large beach-side car park, as well as toilets, a public telephone and a lifeguard station which is manned from late June to early September. There's also a camp site next to the beach and a Youth Hostel just below Carn Llidi.

Speaking of which, if you have the time and energy, then why not continue your walk beyond the beach up onto the summit? Carn Llidi provides unparalleled views of St David's and the surrounding area, and rounds off this beautiful walk in style.

Wye Valley

Near: Chepstow
Ordnance Survey Grid Reference ST 532943
OS Explorer Map OL14

Derek says...

This walk is spectacular and takes you through some of the finest countryside in Monmouthshire. It follows the route of the Wye Valley and boasts a Norman castle, mysterious woods, lots of wildlife and the stunning Tintern Abbey. Plus the Eagle's Nest: a viewing platform standing seven hundred feet above the Wye on the towering Wynd Cliff.

The way up is a bit steep, the views as well as the steps will take your breath away. You'll see Chepstow racecourse, both Severn bridges, Chepstow Castle and – on a fine day – it is said you can see seven counties!

In the spring it passes through stunning bluebell woods but is also beautiful in autumn. It's also possible to break it up into smaller chunks and even miss some of the steps by parking below the Eagle's Nest. If you're lucky you may see a peregrine falcon and the rare red kite which are now established in the Wye Valley. While along the river, look out for heron, kingfisher and otters.

At the end, take a look around the Abbey or the Castle: these are special places that really bring the past to life.

This route along the Wye Valley from Chepstow to Tintern is not only fascinating but dramatic. Start at the leaping salmon waymark in the romantic ruins of Chepstow Castle. After ascending a path through the Castle Dell it is not far to the old Piercefield Estate, where the route passes through ancient woodland and takes in a number of historic viewpoints. The steeply-wooded sides of this impressive gorge have remained virtually untouched by man since trees first colonised the slopes after the ice age.

The central part of this walk, below the Wyndcliff, passes through more woods containing a uniquely high proportion of native yew trees.

The highlight is the ascent of around 365 steps to the Eagles' Nest viewpoint 700 feet above the river. It provides astonishing views back towards Chepstow Castle and over the Wye as it snakes its way down to the Severn Estuary.

From there one continues through Minepit Wood, where iron ore was extracted by the Romans and then down through Limekiln Wood along an old packhorse route to Tintern. The village is world famous for its Cistercian Abbey, once a centre of monastic life for four hundred years.

Chris Barber
Walking Wales Magazine

Start

The Welsh tourism industry is by no means a modern phenomenon. People have been coming here to walk and wander through the beautiful countryside for longer than most of us imagine.

Take the unspoilt splendour of the Wye Valley, for instance. It's a popular destination for walkers today, but over 200 years ago it was arguably a much hotter attraction for ramblers. Back then, walkers came to follow quite literally in the footsteps of the great and the good of their day.

Thanks to artists such as Turner, who painted the castle at Chepstow, and poets such as Wordsworth (who wrote his famous 'Lines Composed Above Tintern Abbey' here in 1798), this lower stretch of the Wye became a popular destination for the 18th century 'in crowd'. They were

Chepstow Castle from the first of Valentine Morris's viewing points

drawn here by the rise of the new Romantic movement, a philosophy that encouraged people to appreciate the natural beauty of the British countryside. Until then, beauty was judged on classical lines derived from Roman and Greek models, but the Romantics wanted to make people appreciate the natural beauty found all around us.

This enthusiasm for home-grown beauty was also helped by the Napoleonic Wars. The conflict meant that young aristocrats who previously would have been sent on Grand Tours of Europe were now staying away from a politically hostile and dangerous continent. Instead, they were exploring Britain and – thanks to the foresight of a young landowner called Valentine Morris – many of them ended up in Chepstow.

Morris' father, also called Valentine, was a plantation owner who had bought the Piercefield estate in Chepstow for just £8,000 back in 1736. Within two years of acquiring Piercefield, he died, passing the estate, along with his sugar plantations in Antigua, to his 15 year old son. Valentine junior saw the potential in the area and began to build scenic walks through his grounds. He built special themed viewing points, some of which were accompanied by fanciful grottos or other follies, all aimed at encouraging the well-to-do to wander through these woods and enjoy the scenery.

His work at Piercefield never paid off however. The costs of running the estate, coupled with gambling and other debts, ruined Valentine, who had to sell his home and retire to the West Indies.

The bulk of the walk that he built here is more or less intact, although much of it is overgrown, making it difficult to appreciate those famous views. As for the follies, many of them have disappeared or fallen into disrepair and are a sad reminder of the estate's heyday. The same goes for Piercefield House. You can just about see it as you wander through the first section of the walk, but you can't visit it. It's owned by Chepstow racecourse (in fact the race track is in what would have been Valentine's back garden!) and as such it's now on private property. It's still standing, but it's mostly the front of the old house which remains more or less intact.

Piercefield House

The former ice house and some of the other buildings are also in ruins, but still visible, although the whole structure is potentially unsafe. If you were to go near it you would see fences keeping people back from the house itself. Piercefield passed through a succession of owners after Morris's day and gradually fell into ruin, as was the fate of many other great houses. Further damage was done during the 1940s when American troops, billeted near Chepstow during the war, used the house for target practice. In fact, the front of the house still bears the bullet holes and battle scars of this unfriendly fire.

The rise and fall of Piercefield House is just a small part of the history covered by this walk. From start to finish, the walk covers Iron Age and Roman settlements, the Norman conquest of Britain, the dissolution of the monasteries and the Industrial Revolution. Not only that, but the path runs parallel to Offa's Dyke, on the other side of the river. It all adds to the value of the area for walking, although we chose it as one of our spring walks because of another one of its selling points – the fantastic abundance of bluebells that you'll find here! We have more wild bluebells in Britain than anywhere else, and a walk through a wood like this in April, with the plants in full fragrant bloom, is a real treat. Unfortunately, it's a treat which is under threat – from foreign plants and from global warming. Spanish bluebells which have been bought to stock our back gardens are now invading the traditional wild bluebell beds. Not only that, the milder winters mean other plants, which normally have to wait until the bluebells have vanished before it's warm enough for them to grow, can now bloom earlier and compete with them. All the more reason, therefore, not to pick any when you do see them!

So how do you get into these woods to enjoy all this flora, fauna and history? Well, the walk starts off at Chepstow Castle, so the path is very easy to find! The castle was built by the Normans in 1067 and stands as a magnificent guardian to this gateway to Wales. It protected the port of Chepstow, and its strategic importance is underlined by the fact that it was one of the first castles in Britain to be built in stone. It's also useful in that if a spring shower washes out your walk, you can pay a visit here or else check out the museum on the opposite side of the road. If you do go inside the castle, walk along the wall above the river and look up to the Eagle's Nest viewing platform, high above you to your left, on the Wynd Cliff. This is where you'll be heading and it'll give you an idea of how high you're going to get.

The Wye walk is signposted from the castle, and although the full walk – which runs from Chepstow to Plynlimon – is 136 miles in length, don't panic, ours is a much more foot-friendly 9 miles! You can also cheat a little at the start. For example, the first hundred yards or so take you past the castle battlements and into the Dell, a lovely green space behind the main streets of Chepstow, and then up onto the main road. You then head for the Leisure Centre where the walk proper begins.

If, however, you have a car, you may be tempted to look around the castle, and then drive straight to the Leisure Centre – it saves you an uphill walk along the roadside and sets you off a lot more quickly. The path disappears behind the local school before emerging through a hole in the wall of the old Piercefield House estate. It's a bit like entering a secret garden – you almost feel that you shouldn't be in there – but from this point on you can wander through beautiful Welsh woodland as the path clings to and climbs along the cliff side above the Wye.

Almost immediately you come across the first of Valentine's viewpoints, called the Alcove. It has clearly seen better days, and although there is a bench here it had been vandalised when we visited. The local authority and the Forestry Commission are now trying to clear the path and free up some of the views, but you will have to use your imagination when walking around the estate, as parts of it are very overgrown and uncared for. Still, you do get a great view of the town and river from here. The Wye is tidal and is also a remarkably clean river too. It supports a wide variety of plant, fish and wildlife – including rare snails, molluscs and crustaceans like the Atlantic stream crayfish. Over thirty different species of fish have been recorded in the Wye, making it one of the most important river systems in Northern Europe, while the clean water and good riverbank cover favours animals such as otters, the rare polecat and 10 out of the 15 species of British bat.

Leaving the Alcove you head straight into the best of the bluebell woods. In April and May this woodland is carpeted with the beautiful little flowers, and if you want a taste of spring this is the place to come to. It's not just the bluebells that makes this a colourful wildlife walk; white flowered garlic can be found throughout the route, and if you can't see the plants then you'll smell them as you wander by. One of the more bizarre-looking signs of spring is the sporadic patches of tooth wort that spring up under the trees. A parasite, it taps off the roots of other plants (we found one living off a laburnum). It gets its name because the odd shaped, pasty white flowers that hang from the stem look like bunches of human teeth.

As the path winds up and around the slopes along the Wye you'll discover some more of those famous viewing points, the next one being a stone platform called, rather disappointingly perhaps, 'The Platform'. It's in a sorry state and its condition more or less sums up the problem with the whole Piercefield Park site. Yew trees have grown up through the middle of the platform, while other species have sprung up in front of it, surrounding the space and blocking your view. Even if you do manage to climb onto it and stand on the spot where the poets and artists stood 200 years ago, you won't see anything except tree trunks and branches.

So the viewing points are in disrepair and the views they were meant to celebrate have been obliterated. Some of Valentine's follies, such as the Druid's Stone, need little or no maintenance, but when you walk into the Grotto, for example, you do wish that someone would spend some time and money restoring these relics to something resembling their former glory.

Derek in the Grotto

Speaking of relics from the walk's past, in a clearing before the final viewpoint there is a huge hole dug right next to the path. This is all that remains of an excavation organised by a wealthy American philanthropist called Dr Orville Owen. He believed that not only were Shakespeare's plays written by Bacon, but that a folio containing these manuscripts was buried near the river Wye. In 1909 he arrived in Chepstow and began two digs – one in the river bank and one on the cliffs above. His arrival was greeted with acres of newspaper print, and to intense press excitement he set about excavating over 700 tons of earth from eight separate holes. His efforts were in vain, however, and he returned home empty handed.

From here on, the path slowly climbs higher and you begin to leave the denser areas of woodland behind and glimpse the Wye below you through the trees. It's a magnificent river, rated as the most beautiful stretch of water in Wales. It's also totally unpolluted and is a designated Site of

Special Scientific Interest from source to mouth. Some walkers divide this route into three sections; the first one ends at the Giant's Cave, the last of Morris's follies. This was a natural cave found on the estate, which Morris had his men blast through to create a tunnel and so continue the walk. It was called the Giant's Cave because a carved stone giant was erected above the entrance, although he fell into the river gorge below years ago.

If you choose to continue on from here, your walk takes you through a younger forest, across a babbling stream and up towards the main road and picnic area. Again, an astute walker may have arranged a lift back to Chepstow from here – but if you really want to appreciate one of the best views in South Wales, cross the main road and follow the signs for the Eagle's Nest and the 365 steps it takes to get you there. Before you hit the steps there's one more treat to enjoy – a small ancient yew-filled forest that feels like a lost world. The yews arch, bend and split open to create a twisted tangle of trees that you pick your way through to get to the Steps. It's a fairytale forest, made for hobbits and hobgoblins, and 60 years ago it would have led to Moss Cottage, a little thatched house which also appeared to belong to a Brothers Grimm fairy tale. Moss Cottage was the entrance to the

Steps and the Eagle's Nest above and our guide, Chris Barber, remembers being taken there as a child by his father. The old lady who lived there charged people to go through her garden and get to the steps. And on the way back down she served the family tea and cake in her back garden.

Unfortunately, this magical little cottage was demolished back in the 1960s so now there's no stopping-off point before the climb, just a sign pointing you in the right direction. In fact, if it wasn't for Chris, the Steps could have suffered the same fate as the Cottage. Back in the late 1960s he wrote an article in the local paper in which he described his search for the steps he remembered from his childhood, and how he found them overgrown and abandoned. The article prompted people like the Lower Wye Valley Preservation Society to revive the path and restore the steps for

The river Wye seen from the Eagle's Nest

public use again. Over the years other volunteers have also helped clear the way (even the army even lent a hand at one point) and their tireless efforts have really paid off.

There are other ways of getting to the Eagle's Nest – in fact, there's a road which takes you almost to the top of the Wynd Cliff – and leads to a car park with a gentle 10 minute walk to the back of the viewing platform. But if you can, try and avoid the temptation to cheat. Grit your teeth and do it the hard way. There's a real sense of achievement to be gained from making it up those famous steps, and you'll soon forget the effort it takes to get there when you finally see the majestic views from the top.

From here you can see both Severn Bridges and the castle, which appears as a tiny garrison in the distance. You also get an amazing view of the whole of Chepstow racecourse, home of the Welsh Grand National. You can also see where the River Wye runs into the Severn and this meeting of the two rivers is the traditional end to the mammoth 136 mile long Wye River Route.

Finally, before you get too carried away – be warned, the view isn't what it was. You used to be able to see nine counties from here, but thanks to local government reorganisation you'll now only see seven!

It's at the Eagle's Nest that some walkers decide to call it a day – maybe it's the effect of all those steps – and so the Wynd Cliff marks the end of the shorter middle section of the walk. From here you could turn back down the main road towards St Arvan's, but we pressed onwards towards Tintern and the beautiful Abbey.

The final stretch of the path is about a mile and a half long and gently takes you back down through more woodland, past more bluebells and white flowered garlic, towards the village of Tintern. As the footpath bends back on itself you get a fantastic view of the Abbey. Established by the Cistercians back in the 12th century and built on successively for the next 400 years, it was shut down by King Henry VIII in 1536. It's now rated as one of the finest ecclesiastical remains in Europe, and a visit around this peaceful giant of a ruin is a great end to the walk.

However, if you still feel the need to keep on walking, try crossing the Wye from the old Iron Bridge and walk back to Chepstow from the English side of the river, down the Offa's Dyke path. Whatever you decide to do, remember that this walk offers just a small taste of what's on offer in this magnificent river valley. Walk just a stretch of it once and you may find yourself smitten. And whether you choose to idle along its paths with watercolours and an easel, like the Romantics of Wordsworth's time, or go hell-for-leather down the Wye from source to mouth like today's 'uber-walkers', this river will reward you time and time again.

Tintern Abbey

Llanthony Priory

Near: Abergavenny
Ordnance Survey Grid Reference SO 288278
OS Explorer Map OL13

Derek says...

This walk is great if you want to relax in a peaceful part of Monmouthshire. It links with the Offa's Dyke National Trail and takes you through some beautiful countryside. There is history, wonderful scenery and lots of plant and animal life too.

The walk starts at Llanthony Priory snuggled deep in the secluded Ewyas valley at the foot of the Black Mountains. There really is a mystical feel about the place – imagine being here at night with a full moon casting a spooky shadow on the ruins. The remains of the Priory are open to the public and are well worth looking around. There is also a pub where you can grab a bite to eat and don't forget to have a look at the information kiosk in the car park – it's connected to the internet so you can check the latest weather forecast for the Black Mountains. Skirrid and Sugarloaf Mountain are close by but for me the best and most breathtaking views are from the top of Hatterall Hill – on a good day you can see as far as the Malvern Hills and Long Mynd in Shropshire. Wonderful!

The Llanthony Valley has long attracted those in search of peace and inspiration. From St David himself to the Augustinian canons who built the magnificent 12th century priory, and the English romantic artists and writers who visited in the 18th Century, all have been drawn by the stunning natural setting. It is not hard to see why!

Our route starts at the atmospheric ruins of the priory and climbs through fields of sheep and cattle to the rough grazing of the common land above. Here it is possible to take a shortcut back to the priory, but it's really worth the extra effort of the climb onto Hatterall Ridge. On a clear day you can stand here on the English border and look east to the Cotswold escarpment, or west to the wild moorlands of the Welsh hills. But sitting in the heather with ravens tumbling and cronking above, the best view is back down to Llanthony itself. The full splendour of this narrow valley, carved by glaciers into the red sandstone rocks of the Black Mountains, is breathtaking and you can't help but ponder on all the history that has gone before.

Mike Scruby *Brecon Beacons National Park*

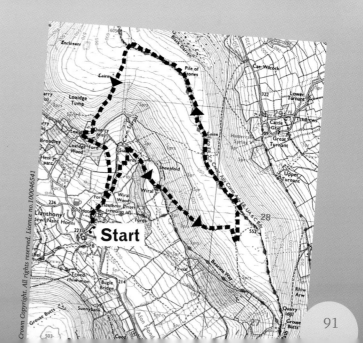

Start

91

The final Spring walk continues our ecclesiastical theme and is another route that proved popular with the Romantic artists – although these days it's also home to horse riders and hard-core hikers!

Just like Tintern Abbey, the ruins of Llanthony Priory were also painted by Turner, as well as by a host of other artists over the years, although the ruins here are less well-preserved and on a much smaller scale. Tintern may have had more attention over the years, but Llanthony has a charm and attraction all its own, which is equally powerful and enthralling.

The Priory itself is a magical place and slightly off the beaten track. It's twelve miles from Abergavenny, off the A465 and nestled deep in the heart of the Black Mountains. The route here has all the ingredients of a good walk: lots of variety in the landscape, a choice of paths to suit all weathers and abilities, and a pub and somewhere to eat at the end of it! There's also a free car park with an electronic information booth that gives you all the latest weather and walking information too.

This is a real magnet for walkers. For example, once a year the Priory acts as the meeting point for the annual Big Black Mountain Challenge, which is held in aid of the nearby Longtown Mountain rescue team. The event attracts around a thousand walkers and features three different sponsored walks, ranging from an epic 26-mile trek to a slightly less demanding 10-mile option. You may be relieved to learn that our route is half that shorter distance again, and it can easily be done in around three hours. Not only that, but there are gentler paths that can be taken around it – so those walkers who are not keen on steep climbs and ridge walks can still find something to do here.

This is arguably one of the most stunning valleys in the eastern section of the Beacons Park, with the Abbey providing a fantastic backdrop to your journey. So if you want a walk that is loaded with eye-candy scenery, littered with 'Kodak moments' and strong on spirituality, then this is the one for you.

The walk starts and ends at the historic Priory. The Christian association with the area goes back a long way, with St David allegedly building a cell here back in the 6th century. It fell into disrepair and was abandoned to the wilds, but some 600 years later – during the reign of William Rufus, son of William the Conqueror – a Norman knight called William de Lacey, who had got lost while on a hunting trip, stumbled across it. Something about the place moved him to mend his ways and take on a life of piety, and by 1108 he had organised a monastic settlement and built the first priory here. The Augustinian order that he established was forever tainted by association with the 'English' monarchy however and the Priory became a target of endless Welsh frustration and anger. Because of that, it endured some turbulent times and had to be rebuilt between 1175 and 1230. It's the ruins of this building that can be seen today.

Looking back at the priory five minutes into the walk

The border region was always quite lawless, and maintaining the institution here was never easy or particularly safe – which is ironic when you consider that those wild Welsh hills that laid siege to the Priory also provided the order with plenty of spiritual inspiration. A walk to the ridges above them was to 'climb up and touch heaven', according to many writers of the time. Not only that, but the monks lived beneath a naturally occurring crucifix shape formed by the hills to the east of the priory, Bâl Bach, Bâl Mawr, Bwlch Isaf and Bwlch Bachare. However, while the monks may have built their holy house in the shadow of this 'cross', it offered them little protection. From the 13th century onwards, the canons here were continually harassed and attacked – and even murdered. In 1399 Owain Glyndŵr's rebellion led to the area being occupied by Welsh rebels, and this weakened the Priory's authority and wealth even further. Finally, in 1538, King Henry VIII brought its long religious history to an end, claiming it as his own and then selling it for £160 to the Chief Justice of Ireland. It has stayed in private ownership ever since, although the medieval arches still stand and the opportunity to climb and touch heaven still exists.

To take advantage of that esoteric opportunity, all you have to do is follow the signs and walk from the car park, passing the Priory on your right and then head out through the farm gate towards Hatterall Hill. From here there are two ways of doing this walk. You can either leave the farm then head straight up the steep path to Loxidge Tump, walking along the Offa's Dyke path on top of the ridge, before meeting the Beacon's Way path which slowly winds down back to the Priory. Or you can cut across the farm, through the ruins of the poet Walter Savage Landor's house at Siarpal, meet the Beacon's Way route just after Wiral wood, then head

up the gentle slope to the ridge and do the reverse walk along Offa's Dyke, back to Loxidge and down again to the Priory.

We chose the latter, because it's initially easier, gives you more chance to admire the woods and farmland in springtime, and because you get to see what's left of Siarpal House and learn about its eccentric former owner.

Much of the land at the bottom of the valley is traditional farming pasture owned by the same families for generations. There is a permanency to the place that seems to have overwhelmed all visitors to the area, from the monks of the Priory to the artists' colony at nearby Capel-y-ffin, founded by the sculptor and painter Eric Gill in the early 1900s. That never flourished, and neither did the grand designs of the poet Walter Savage Landor.

Originally from Warwickshire, he was a wayward young man – expelled from Rugby School for insolence and expelled from Oxford for shooting someone! A restless soul, the poet and writer came here in the early 1800s and fell in love with the valley, believing it to be the perfect Romantic rural idyll. In 1809 he sold off the family assets to buy the Priory estate and build a large new house. But within three years he was gone, with his house never completed, a jumble of stray walls and random foundations his only legacy.

Landor upset the locals, falling out with them over rents, and on one occasion getting thrown out of a window for his troubles. He also fell foul of several law suits, all of which conspired to send him packing to the continent. Even the horse chestnut trees he planted have died; they lie on the path like bleached and tangled bony relics, abandoned by the land.

You pass his intended home as the route turns right and slowly begins to rise. Here the landscape begins to change from pasture to woodland. This is one of the reasons why we chose this as a Spring walk. While the Wye Valley may be filled with bluebells, it's hard sometimes – when you're actually surrounded by the forest – to get a sense of the trees bursting into life. To put it crudely, you can't see the trees for the forest. On this route, the walk and the farmland allow you to get some distance, to stand back and appreciate the new fresh greens flooding through into life. And it's that perspective the sloping hills allow here – a perspective which has continued to draw landscape painters to the area for the past 200 years.

Really this is a place (and a walk) that allows you to admire the bigger picture. The trail takes you up past a beautifully restored farmhouse and then disappears into the woods again (although there is a signposted junction near here where those wanting a shorter, less demanding walk can head back down to the Priory). 107. The path up to the ridge is in good condition, particularly when you realise that not only does it experience heavy walking traffic but that it's also used by pony trekkers too (and you'll probably pass a few riders before your walk is finished).

It's at this point that you join the Beacon's Way route which, as we mentioned in our Skirrid walk, is a trail that runs from the Holy Mountain of the Skirrid to Bethlehem in the far west of the National Park. It normally takes about 8 days to complete that particular walk, so you'll be relieved to discover that we only use it for a mile. It's from here, as the path rises more sharply, that you begin to get fantastic views of the Priory behind you and the Sugar Loaf mountain dead ahead. From this point on, the view down the valley to Cwmyoy just gets better and better.

It's a beautiful U-shaped valley, carved out by glaciers over 50,000 years ago; it shows all the classic signs of that ice flow erosion, from the steep sides to the occasional huge slump of land, as in the tump above Cwmyoy (visible to the left of the valley as you look down the path). This was caused by the support from the glacier literally melting away, and the old red sandstone collapsing behind it as it goes. In fact, if you have time, try and visit St Martin's church at Cwmyoy. The crooked old building nestles on the eastern slope of the valley; its odd angles and twisted walls perfectly mirror the subsidence and the slipped, slumped earth below its foundations.

As the path gets steeper you rise above the tree line and start walking into moorland. The hills here are home to grouse, and the Park allows shooting of the birds in exchange for help from the hunters in maintaining the habitat up here. It seems odd that a conservation agency should allow even small-scale shooting of birds, but the fees from the hunters and their manpower are much needed. It's the only way to maintain the correct environment for the grouse to live here – and what benefits the grouse also helps whinchats, stonechats, pippets, skylarks and curlews, to name but a few of the birds you'll see on the top of the ridge.

The other big attraction up here is the heather, although to appreciate it fully you'll need to return in late summer and early autumn when it blooms and turns the top of the mountains purple.

At the top of the Offa's Dyke Path, at the apex of the ridge that runs along the mountain, you'll be rewarded for that long climb with some simply stunning views. The ridge rises to 800 metres (around 2,000 feet) here, and while it's not the highest point of the walk you do get some amazing views. On a good day you'll see the Cotswold Escarpment over the Malvern Hills and, as you follow the path along, the Shropshire Hills too.

This path forms the border between England and Wales, and from this view it really does look like two different countries – what with the green patchwork-squared quilt of the Longtown Valley to your right, and the brooding, heather-covered tops of the Black Mountains to your left.

Despite the history with Offa, there is very little in the way of archaeological interest here. The Dyke is not fortified at this point and instead relies on the natural barrier of the ridge. There are remnants of Iron Age cairns along the ridge which were probably burial mounds, and Bronze Age artefacts have also been discovered here. There are also some later small-scale excavations which were probably caused by quarrying for roof stone. It may not amount to much, but it's enough to remind you that this wilderness has been inhabited for a long, long time – probably since the last Ice Age when it was populated by early hunter-gatherers. These sparse, often dislocated, remnants of our relationship with this landscape are capable of elevating the walk to something quite special and, at times, intoxicating. You follow the ridge for just over a mile and those spellbinding views get better and better as the path rises a hundred metres or so.

Then you have to face the inevitable walk down. Coming back, you can either tackle the steep climb down at Loxidge, or drop down through Cwm Siarpal. Either way returns you to the main path back to the Priory. Perhaps unsurprisingly, it's on the way back that the beauty of the ruin properly reveals itself. Some people will tell you that the best time to do this walk is in late afternoon, leaving you to approach the Priory just as the evening is ushered in. And that it's at this time that you'll best experience the sense of spirituality that attracted those early pilgrims here.

There is no doubt that this is a unique little corner of Wales; you might just find that it's so special that you may wish to return here again to appreciate the valley in all the seasons.

Summer

Barafundle/Stackpole

Near: Pembroke
Ordnance Survey Grid Reference SR 967931
OS Explorer Map OL36

Derek says…

I've been to Tenby and Saundersfoot a few times but never to this part of the Pembrokeshire peninsula before. So despite recovering from a nasty dose of chickenpox, I was quite excited at the prospect of doing this walk.

Part of the walk is through a MoD firing range but don't let this put you off. The scenery along the coast is breathtaking and try to visit the historic chapel at St Govan's Head. It's a steep climb but while you are there you can always pray for good weather!

The golden sandy beach at Broad Haven South is beautiful and then just around the corner are the fabulous lily ponds at Bosherston Lake, a haven for plants and wildlife. The water here is clear and full of life. The best bit, though, has to be the wonderful beach at Barafundle Bay. It's so peaceful and quiet here: unspoilt by the twenty-first century, making it a perfect spot for a summer picnic. When you reach Stackpole Quay you can treat yourself in the café and if you're feeling tired catch a bus back to St Govan's!

This walk has everything: stunning scenery, dramatic cliffs, history, archaeology, amazing lily ponds and fantastic beaches. And it constantly changes with time and tide, weather and seasons.

Watch the acrobatic antics of the chough, smell the fishy cliff-nesting sites of the razorbills and guillemots or the sweeter smell of wild honeysuckle and feel the historic atmosphere within St Govan's Chapel, nestling in a steep sided cliff.

The majority of this walk is flat with steeper climbs to and from the beaches. It can be walked in one stretch of 9.5 km or broken down into manageable chunks using the local bus service.

And, if like Derek, you enjoy visiting local tea rooms, then you're in for a treat as there's a great one at Stackple Quay!

Lynne Ferrand
Pembrokeshire Coast National Park

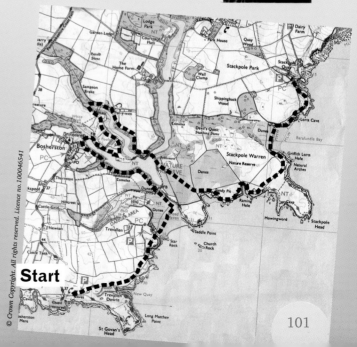

Start

I'm not sure why, but all three of our summer walks have one obvious thing in common – they're all based around large bodies of fresh water. Maybe it's because a Welsh summer will leave you parched and thirsty – or, more realistically, wet and washed out! Either way, these are all walks you can tackle whatever the weather and whatever your ability.

The first of these summertime specials is the Stackpole Estate, an 810-acre National Nature Reserve packed with landmarks and outstanding features. Stackpole was the summer retreat of the Scottish Cawdor family, who created the lily ponds at Bosherton Lakes and the harbour at

Stackpole Quay. In all, the clan owned 17,735 acres of land in Pembrokeshire (and over 33,000 acres in Camarthenshire too) and their house, known as Stackpole Court, was one of the finest in Britain. But while it was grand enough to host Edward VII in 1902, within sixty years it had fallen into such a poor state of repair that it was demolished.

The Stackpole estate is now owned by the National Trust, although it's another major landowner in the area that you'll be most aware of when you begin the walk.

Our route starts in the car park above St Govan's, and driving there you'll see signs warning you about the Ministry of Defence firing range next door. The main firing range is at Castlemartin, and lots of people head there to watch the Warriors and other assault vehicles go through their paces – in fact, the

Action Man!

Army has even set aside a designated viewing platform for tank spotters. And while this does mean that the land immediately around this dangerous area is closed for about 60% of the year, don't worry – the firing rarely affects visitors to St Govan's. The disruption here normally amounts to no more than 20 or 30 road closures a year due to training manoeuvres. So while the warning signs, barriers, red flags and control points may look a little intimidating, you are perfectly safe on the path we've chosen; even if the sound of distant gunfire can seem a little surreal at times. And despite their best efforts, the army can't succeed in disturbing the peace of the little chapel here, tucked away as it is below the cliff tops, facing the sea.

As you walk down the 70 or so stone steps to it, you immediately forget about the 21st century and all the distant rumblings that furnish it. I say 70 or so steps, because legend has it that no-one can accurately count the number. If you visit here in a group, try to count them independently and compare your totals at the end. Few walkers ever agree on the same figure,

Tucked into the cliffside, the magical chapel of St Govan's

but that's probably due to the jumble of lumps, bumps, half steps and true steps that you find along the way, rather than any supernatural force being at work. That said, though, this is a magical place where the sound of the ocean crashing in front of the chapel window drowns out the rude noises of the firing ranges above.

The chapel was definitely here in the 11th century, and it could possibly date all the way back to the 6th century. It is a remarkable little building, wedged as it is between the rocks and battered by the elements. It is dedicated to St Govan, who died in 586. Originally from County Wexford, Gobhan – or Gobban, as his name would have been spelled – was an Abbot who, legend has it, was visiting the area when he was attacked and chased by pirates. They hounded him over the cliff tops and he seemed to be doomed until a higher power came to his rescue. As the pirates were about to catch him, a cleft miraculously opened up in the rock. He climbed into this unnatural fissure which then magically closed over him. Once the pirates had gone away, it opened again and the Abbot was released. To give thanks for the protection shown to him, he vowed to stay in the area, preaching and doing God's work.

The chapel itself is very small (just 5.3 metres by 3.8) and simply made. It used to have a well near the main entrance, and the water here – which has to be scooped out with a small spoon or sea shell – is allegedly blessed with healing properties. Legend has it that it can cure eye complaints, skin diseases and rheumatic problems – not that any of our team tried it. Outside there is a large boulder known as the Bell Rock which is said to contain a silver bell. It was put there after pirates (them again!) had taken the bell from the chapel tower. St Govan prayed for its return, and when the angels retrieved it they made sure it would be safe by placing it inside the rock. Fortunately, when St Govan tapped the rock, the bell still sounded with a note a thousand times stronger than the original, and loud enough to be heard through its stone safety box.

The slope in front of the chapel gives you some great views of St Govan's Head way out to your left. Back on the top path, keep the sea to the right of you and head along the cliffs. Although you're just minutes into the main walk the scenery is breathtaking, and with the waves crashing into the rocks below, you get a real sense of that wild and rugged Welsh coastline. Thanks to a straight, flat, tarmac path which serves the route for the first couple of hundred yards, it's a landscape which is very accessible to all kinds of people – not just hardened walkers.

It's a great place to birdwatch, too, and you should spot choughs, peregrine falcons, guillemots, razorbills, cormorants and shags here. They all nest on the rock face – which

Barafundle Beach seen from the Stackpole Quay side of the bay

causes a few problems because the cliffs here attract climbers as well as sea birds. St Govan's has some of the best sea cliff climbing in Europe, but it's situated within a National Park that has restrictions on cliff access in order to protect birdlife. That's why, as you walk along the cliff top, you may spot little red concrete 'pots' dotted on the edge of the cliffs, like little Tommy Cooper-style fezzes. These are warning markers to keep the climbers away from these sensitive nesting sites during breeding times. Given that these cliffs can be quite treacherous, and that the Coastguards are often called out to rescue stranded climbers (and the occasional sheep that's fallen down), the birds are probably welcome to them!

There are other pressures on this habitat, apart from climbers. If you look out towards St Govan's Head from here, you'll see the results of a spectacular rock fall back in 2005. Cliff erosion is a big problem along the coastal path, and the colossal tumble of rock here shows you just how much damage can be caused by the effects of the wind and sea.

As the path takes you away from the cliff face you'll see some huge concrete bunkers. Although they're not in use today, these sinister, squat buildings were constructed back in the early 1940s for troop training. And if you climb on top of the largest bunker you'll see a perfect stone circle target below it, laid out towards the sea. This was added to the site in the 1960s to help train bomber pilots during the Cold War.

You continue the walk through the target towards Broadhaven Beach – which doesn't seem altogether sensible with the sound of rockets and gunfire in the distance but, trust us, you'll be fine!

Broadhaven Beach is preceded by another car park, and the good thing about this walk is that it's punctuated with lots of pit stops where you can park up and hop from spot to spot if you don't fancy wearing out your shoe leather. There are steps that lead down onto the sands, and Broadhaven itself is a cracking little beach – nice and wide, beautifully clean, and not too crowded. One thing to point out as you do walk along the beach is the huge rock pointing out of the sea, standing, as it does, like a giant 'thumbs up' sign. This is Church Rock, which used to be called Stack Pole (from the Welsh, Stack Pwll, roughly translated as Stack 'pool' or 'inlet') and it was this rock that originally gave the estate its name.

As you wander around the beach to your left, the angle of view changes and you'll see the shape of the rock transforming, becoming more like a petrified church with a steeple – hence the modern name. Walkers tend to wander straight through the beach to get to the next point of interest, Bosherton Lakes, home to the famous Lily Ponds.

The path leads away to your left from Broadhaven, taking you to a small dune system with a wooden footbridge in front of you. From here you cross from the beach into the beautiful green oasis of Bosherton Lakes. In fact, it's just one lake split into three separate arms (the East, Central and Western arms) by a system of dams and pathways over the water. The lakes in summer are a fantastic sight, covered in lilies and teeming with wildlife. There are more than 600 species of flowering plant here, and 70 different species of breeding birds. If you're very lucky, you might see otters here, but you're more likely to spot herons, mallards, kingfishers or one of the 20 species of dragonfly that lazily buzz over the lily pads. The lilies flower in June, which is another reason why this is a great summer walk, and they turn Bosherton into a bewitching water garden, straight out of an Impressionist painting.

Lynne trying to look interested as Derek goes into an impromptu forecast!

You approach the lakes through a sheltered woodland path, which allows you glimpses of the lush watery landscape beyond, through the leafy canopy that closes all around you. It's a lazy, shadow-dappled walk, although you should remember that the twisting path here is a lot longer than it looks and it takes a while to get around all three lakes. The lakes are the jewel in the crown of the Estate and are blessed with extremely clear water. They are fed by an aquifer which, like an underground stream, rises up through the limestone and floods the area.

As the Cawdor family dammed the bottom of the lakes, they trapped this water and created the lake system we see today. The limestone here acts like a colander; as it's porous, it allows the water to rise through and fill the lakes during wet weather and to drain away during a dry spell, so the water levels fluctuate quite a bit. If you're lucky, you'll get to visit here when the lakes are full, leaving the water to lap just below the level of the wooden walkways. It will feel as if you're walking on water and, with the gardens in full bloom and teeming with wildlife, you'll be treated to a truly sumptuous summer spectacle.

Even on a bad day, it is worth just wandering around the lakes. The beautiful arched bridges and the little ruin on top of the Warren are all worth a look, and if you have the time and energy to take in all that's on offer here, you won't regret it. Once you're done with the lakes, you can head back up onto the main coastal walk. On a summer's day it's a glorious stretch, with hidden coves that are home to hundreds of nesting sea birds. However, such are the riches of this stretch of Pembrokeshire, you'll want to hurry through to get to our next destination – Barafundle Bay.

Barafundle Bay is a real hidden gem – which is a bizarre thing to say about a beach regularly described as the best in Britain. One of the reasons why it is a secret pleasure is that there is no road to it – you have to walk to Barafundle and, when you get there, there are no burger vans, bouncy castles, litter, deckchairs for rent, novelty shops, car parks or donkey rides. It's totally unspoilt by the modern world and is all the better for it – a timeless, often deserted, movie-set of a beach. As you drop down through the trees that line the path above Barafundle, you get a hint of those golden sands below. And when you finally hit the bay, you're rewarded with a stretch of sand listed as one of the top 12 beaches in the world by the *Good Holiday Guide*.

Country Life magazine gave it the title of Britain's Best Picnic Spot in an article called 'Perfect Places' – and 'perfect place' just about sums Barafundle up. It goes without saying that it's a Blue Flag Beach, the highest award for beach cleanliness and Pembrokeshire boasts 11 such top-quality beaches in all – more than any other county in Wales. It's a dream of a place and you'll want to idle here, kick off your walking boots and revel in a landscape that seems stolen from our collective imagination, the ideal beach for the kind of summer we rarely get to enjoy.

But this is a book about walking, so we would urge you to fight the temptation to settle into the dunes for the rest of the day and instead carry on up the stone staircase that leads from the beach back up onto the Coastal Path. If you can tear yourself away, it's a fairly short ten-minute walk from Barafundle to Stackpole Quay.

This was a harbour built by the Cawdors to house their yacht and to bring in coal and building materials for their house. The Quay was also used by local businesses. Limestone from the nearby quarry was shipped out from here and it also supported a small fishing industry, which more or less survives today (you'll probably spot the little crab and lobster fishing boats bobbing about outside of the harbour). The National Trust is responsible for the Quay, and in order to safeguard the local boats and their livelihood, they have recently renovated the cambered harbour.

However, you may find that its another relic of the Cawdor family that provides the best treat at the end of this walk. The old coal sheds have been transformed into a great little tea shop with a terrific selection of cakes, and it's the ideal place to end your walk! Also, the coastal bus service picks up here at the Quay – so you can get a ride back to St Govan's.

If you've got plenty of energy left, though, and you fancy walking off those cakes, then you could walk back across the estate, to the lakes and Broadhaven, before retracing your steps to the Church. That route is mainly through pasture and woodland, and while it's not as spectacular as the coastal path it does bring you back into the centre of Stackpole and gives another dimension to the walk.

But whichever way you choose to do this trail, you won't be disappointed. It's a cracking summer's walk, and if you're lucky enough to get to Barafundle on a day when it's all but deserted, you'll find yourself raving about this spot for many years to come.

Elan Valley

Near: Rhayader
Ordnance Survey Grid Reference SN 922644
OS Explorer Map 200

Derek says…

I have long wanted to visit the Elan Valley and so was looking forward to this walk. It is thought by some to be the Lake District of Wales. Its five reservoirs and stone dams make it one of the most scenic areas of mid Wales.

Rainfall is high with around 1830 mm (72 inches) on average a year but the area is a pleasure to visit at any time of year. I went in June, on the Summer solstice, but the weather was more like Autumn: sunshine and blustery showers with a strong and chilly westerly wind. The wind whips through the valley and is squeezed between the hills.

Part of this walk is along the Elan Valley Trail which is easy to follow: a surfaced path, suitable for everyone including people in wheelchairs, pushchairs, cyclists and horse riders. Hanging oak forests, rocky outcrops and farmland make this the best place in the country to see the famous Red Kite. You may see one floating in the air but if not you could always go on a bird safari! Pop into the visitor centre for details.

It's impossible to walk within the Elan Valley and not fall in love with its 72 square miles of upland splendour, captured in this perfect walk. Enjoy the typical Welsh sessile oak woodlands with pied flycatchers, wood warblers and redstarts for company. Each time you take a breather and look back over your shoulder, the views become increasingly spectacular.

Reaching the summit and heading towards the forestry, the breathtaking landscape overlooking Craig Goch reservoir and the hills of the Cambrian mountains comes into view. Whatever the season or the weather, the view from this hilltop remains beautiful. Very often I look down on a red kite gliding over the hillside and fields, the hills are alive with skylark and pipits, and in the forestry nearby, crossbill can frequently be seen. Looking out across the Pen y Garreg Reservoir during haymaking, I had a few sightings of a great dog otter. Below, nestled into the hillside at the foot of the slope, is Troedrhiwdrain, my home.

Sorcha Lewis
Countryside Officer, Elan Valley

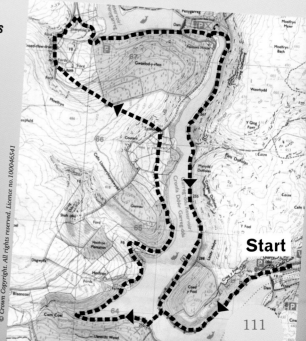

Start

The five reservoirs in the Elan Valley come with an awful lot of land to walk around. Unsurprisingly, then, this is a place that's totally geared up for walkers, with plenty to see and do here.

The route we chose was one of the longest walks we filmed for the series. It takes in three reservoirs, and at 12 miles it could put some people off. But before you panic, remember this – just like all our long walks, this can be broken down into smaller, more foot-friendly paths. In fact, you could easily plan to walk this place one reservoir at a time and still find plenty to enjoy here.

The reservoirs, of course, are man-made and they date back to the early 1890s. They were built to provide clean water for Birmingham, which at that time had suffered outbreaks of water-borne diseases such as typhoid and cholera. The narrow downstream Elan valleys were easy to convert, while the wet climate (there's an average rainfall here of 1803 mm) also proved a distinct advantage. Another naturally occurring boon to the dam builders was the impermeable bedrock that prevented the water seeping away. It all added up to the perfect location and, in 1892, an Act of Parliament was passed, allowing the purchase of the watershed land for the construction of reservoirs.

As a result, all 100 occupants of the Elan Valley were moved out and the villages here abandoned. Only the landowners were compensated and, in all, three manor houses, a school, 18 farms and a church were demolished to make way for the dams. A railway line was constructed to bring in men and building materials into the valley, and it's this track which forms the backbone of the walkers' route around the reservoirs. In fact, the old workshops and locomotive sheds have now been converted into the Elan Valley Visitor Centre, which is where this walk begins.

The Visitor Centre has a great restaurant and café, as well as a number of exhibitions based on the history and wildlife of the area, and is well worth a look before setting off. From the Centre you head up towards Caban Coch dam, the first of the five dams, and one which, when the reservoir is at full capacity, is transformed by any further overfill into a temporary waterfall. Even without the white cascade of water, it's still an awesome sight as you look up to it from the bottom path.

The dam is 37 metres high and has a capacity of 35,530 megalitres (a megalitre = 1,000,000 litres) of water. At its base, Caban Coch is as wide as it is high, and if you could see a cross section of the dam it would look like a huge triangle, standing as it does like a giant stone wedge against the water. This dam supplies the river Elan, and as you walk up the foxglove-covered slope beside it you'll see a series of protruding slabs that look like castle ramparts. These were the support stones for the scaffolding that ran along the top of the dam and carried a little train that travelled back and forth transporting building materials and workers.

It's a peaceful spot today, but in the 1890s this place was a hive of activity. More than 5,000 people worked and lived here during the construction of the dams. They were housed in a specially built village of wooden huts, and new workers had to spend a night in a nearby 'doss house' to be de-loused and checked for infectious diseases before being allowed across the river to join this community. Single men lived in groups of 8, sharing a terraced house with a man and wife. The village boasted a pub, a canteen, a hospital and a bath house; men were allowed to bathe three times a week, but women only once!

At the top of the dam you'll see the main path leading off in front of you, taking you alongside the water's edge. Once you're through the gate you'll see an odd-shaped bench made out of wood and iron railway lines. This is the first of a series of specially designed seats that have been commissioned to mark mile-long stretches of the path. So every time you pass one of these unique benches, you'll know how far you've gone.

The path here is as easy and accessible as you're likely to get. It's

covered in tarmac, so its wheelchair friendly, and you'll see cyclists, parents with prams and people on horseback using this route too.

Experienced walkers may find it a bit easy, even boring, but the views are great and it does get more difficult later on. The only drawback is that from this side of the reservoir you won't be able to see the remains of the Nant y Gro dam; they're on the opposite side of the shore and tucked away into the mountain side. The old ruined dam is of interest because it played an important part in one of the most famous attacks of the Second World War – the Dambusters raid.

The team behind the mission discovered that the little dam at Nant y Gro was a scale replica (exactly one-fifteenth of the size, in fact) of one of the targets in the German Ruhr Valley. So the RAF planners decamped here to experiment with the size of explosive needed to blow the dam up and release the torrent of water behind it. There is an information board on the slope to the side of the ruins telling the story and, even though the damaged walls of Nant y Gro still remain, they are overgrown and slightly hidden.

If you wanted to just walk around Caban Coch reservoir, though, this is one of the things worth looking out for (others include a beautifully restored Welsh Long House and the unfinished Dôl-y-mynach Dam). But on our route, the next landmark you'll see is the green-topped Foel Tower which sits alongside the Garreg Ddu Viaduct. At the Tower you turn left and then walk over the Viaduct (which is also the main road, so watch out for the traffic) and head towards Nantgwyllt Church. The church was built by the Birmingham Corporation to replace the one that was drowned in the valley below. In fact, the bell at the top of church tower is all that remains of the original building.

Of more interest, though, is what's going on under your feet. Beneath the viaduct there's a submerged dam which divides the reservoir. Everything below the tower (that is, all the water towards the Visitor Centre) is cordoned off to supply the river Elan (approximately 123 million litres of water in all). Everything on the other side is all for Birmingham.

Not only that, but the water finds its way down the 73 miles of pipeline to the Midlands without the aid of a pump or any other type of mechanics. Instead it relies on gravity, with the height difference between the Elan Valley and Birmingham (a difference of just 52 metres) enough to push the water along. Apparently, when the water was first turned on, it took a whole week to arrive at its destination!

As the path swings around from the car park next to the church, the landscape begins to change and you enter a lush, green woodland. Look out for the owl nesting boxes on some of the trees. They look like wooden speed cameras and are there to encourage tawny owls to roost in the wood. You'll also see pied flycatchers, spotted flycatchers, wood warblers and redstarts, as well as great spotted woodpeckers and five different species of tit.

In fact, over 180 different bird species have been recorded on the Elan estate since records began in the 1880s. And in 1995 the Countryside Ranger team saw 67 different species on the Estate in one day, during a sponsored bird watch for WaterAid. It should therefore come as no surprise that the Trust runs regular bird watching safaris through the broadleaved woodlands, which themselves are Sites of Special Scientific Interest. The oak here, which is primarily Sessile Oak (a native species which is important and dominant in the hillside woodlands of Wales), also supports hundreds of different types of insects, including the rare cardinal beetle and the purple hairstreak butterfly. There are also 20 species of mammal to be found in the estate, but most are nocturnal creatures and wary of walkers (and other humans!). But if you are lucky you might catch a glimpse of a badger, otter, polecat, weasel or stoat.

You won't be able to see much of Cwm Elan, the old Estate House, though. Owned by the Groves family, it was demolished in 1904 as part of the building of the reservoirs. Little of it survives now, although the path takes you past an old boundary wall and an overgrown hothouse where the family tried to grow peaches and other fruits. In the early 1800s, Cwm Elan became a temporary home to the poet Shelley, who was a cousin of

Thomas Grove Jnr. The family had hoped that spending some time in Wales would calm the young hot-head and radical, and it seems he took a fancy to the area, returning in 1812 with his wife Harriet to settle in the valley at Nantgwyllt. He had hopes of establishing a radical community there, but financial and political circumstances forced the Shelley family out of their home after just 3 months.

As you walk on through the estate, the landscape changes again to uphill farmland, marsh and bog. Again, these are all protected areas. Over seventy square miles of moorland, bog, woodland, river and reservoir in the reserve are identified as having national importance, due to the diversity of the plant life here. Not only that, but the Estate has also been recognised as the most important area for land birds in Wales. Wherever you walk you're in an important and protected environment.

Derek and Sorcha pick through the boggy ground on the way to Tynllidiart farmhouse

The Trust also preserves the architecture of the area. Apart from the Long House, they've also renovated the next building you pass on the walk, the farmhouse of Tynllidiart. This charming white house is rented out as holiday accommodation and enjoys fantastic views over the Garreg Ddu reservoir. For walkers, though, it marks a point where you have to decide whether to follow the gentle path around the reservoir to Pen-y-garreg, the next dam, and then join the main road, or to head for the hills above for a very steep climb that delivers some stunning views.

117

Obviously we headed up and while the gradient might make your thighs burn it really is worth the effort. As you climb high above Tynllidiart you are rewarded with superb views over Garreg Ddu, and your eye can also follow the sweep of the old railway line along the water's edge. You'll also see one bare, brown mountainside that sticks out like a sore thumb amongst the lush, green-covered mountains and woodland. This is part of a project by the Trust to remove some of the pine forests and replace them with Welsh oak, planted with acorns harvested from the land around the reservoirs.

As you continue up and over, you'll find the wind beginning to whip around you – so take care. Remember, up here you're very exposed and, the stronger the wind, the bigger the chill factor – so be aware of the cold when packing your rucksack. As you emerge over the brow of the hill you'll be faced with some truly awe-inspiring scenery. The view from here stops you in your tracks, with Pen-y-garreg reservoir with its tell-tale island in the middle laid out before you and above it Craig Goch, the highest of the five dams. You'll also see the Cambrian Mountains in the distance, and on a clear, sunny day you'll feel as if you're on top of the world, blessed just to be here.

After all that hard climbing, you'll be glad to learn that the walk down is fairly gentle and gives you plenty of opportunity to get your breath back and take in the scenery. You'll also pass through farmland, so remember to be respectful and to keep in mind that, while it's a beautiful landscape, it's also a working one. One other thing to think about is this: the farm here gets its electricity from a generator and its water from a spring on the hill above. So even though they're surrounded by millions of gallons of water and all that hydro-electric power, they can't enjoy any of it. It doesn't seem fair, does it?

As you pass down through the farm, you're met with another choice. Do you head up to Craig Goch or back down to Pen-y-garreg? We went back towards Pen-y-garreg, taking in one of the many spectacular flower meadows along the way.

Summer is the time to see these in all their glory. Eight species of orchid grow in the estate and you'll also find eyebright, upright vetch, butterwort and sundews, to name but a few. The flowers are a reminder that, even when faced with spectacular views all around you, sometimes it's also worth looking at your feet!

As you get to the dam at Pen-y-garreg you're faced with a long 5-mile walk back to the Visitor Centre. You may be lucky and get to catch the Post Bus here, which can take you back, but as it only runs once a day it's not really a safe bet. However, there are plenty of car parks along the way – so if you don't fancy a long march back, then some forward planning is recommended.

Nearing the end of the walk through the flower meadow above Pen-y-garreg

If you do decide to proceed on foot, then this last leg gives you lots of opportunities to admire the railway workings, more of those marvellous park benches, and the cooling quality of the stiff breezes that blow down the valley, across the top of the water. It will also drive home just how much there is to see here and how many little paths and minor routes there are to explore and enjoy.

The Visitor Centre has a pack of alternative walks that you can do, and this is the sort of place that walkers can keep coming back to, time and time again, whatever the season.

Llangorse Lake

Near: Brecon
Ordnance Survey Grid Reference SO 128272
OS Explorer Map OL13

Derek says…

I've been to Llangors Lake a few times over the years, indeed a friend taught me how to water ski there in the late 1980s. Mind you, I think I spent more time in the water than on it! It's a popular place, especially in summer, but this walk does take you away from the crowds.

The walk begins at the jetty in front of the crannog and it's worth taking a look around the new visitor centre. This wooden building standing on stilts with a witchlike pointed thatched roof looks like something out of a Harry Potter movie.

After feeding the ducks and swans on the water's edge, you progress across rolling farm pasture which can flood following heavy rain. When you reach Tŷ Mawr farm, look out for a giant Vietnamese pot-bellied pig!

It's a steep climb to the top of Allt yr Esgair but worth the effort. There is a wonderful view of the lake from the summit and on a clear day you can see the Black Mountains and the Brecon Beacons in the distance, so if you do follow in my footsteps, be sure to bring your camera!

Llangorse Lake, the largest natural lake in south Wales, has a wealth of history and wildlife interest. Visit the Crannog Centre on the lake shore and discover some of the secrets of the lake before you set off.

The walk itself can be split into two parts. The first is a gentle walk around the western end of the lake to the fields below Tŷ Mawr Farm. This is best done in early summer when the flower rich meadows are blooming, butterflies are on the wing and the reedbeds are full of the chatter of warblers. In the winter, when the lake level rises, this path is often flooded.

You can continue beside the lake to the beautiful church at Llangasty, but those of a more energetic disposition should follow the path up onto Allt yr Esgair. The short, steep climb is rewarded with one of the best views in the National Park. Right on the summit lie the remains of a Bronze Age burial cairn. From here the Brecon Beacons stretch away to the west and the Black Mountains to the east with the jewel of Llangorse Lake shining below. It is not hard to see why our ancestors should have chosen this as a last resting place!

Mike Scruby
Brecon Beacons
National Park

121

The final route is a long meandering climb that delivers arguably the best view in the Brecon Beacons and which turns this mile-long lake into a single blue teardrop in a glorious green landscape.

It's also a walk that weaves its way through time, from Ice Age Wales to the Middle Ages, and from Elizabethan lords and ladies, back to Iron Age warriors. It's also packed with wildlife, including the birds which live off the 153 hectares of water and the insects that buzz and crawl around the protected wildflower meadows you pass on the climb to Allt yr Esgair, our final destination.

Llangorse is easy to find. The lake, the second largest in Wales (only Bala is bigger) also gives its name to a pretty village which hugs the shoreline eight miles outside Brecon, just off the A40 main road. Nestled in the Brecon Beacons National Park (which also boasts Wales' highest lake, Llyn y Fan Fawr), the area is a hugely popular centre for water sports, wildlife watching and walking.

Over 50,000 people a year visit Llangorse and while it's one of the big 'honey pot sites' in the park, most of the crowds and activities are centred around the five miles of shoreline. So all you need to do to avoid the crowds is to take a route like this one, which takes you through some evocative scenery with plenty to see and do.

Like the majority of our walks, Llangorse offers you an easy-to-find starting point with car parking, plenty of amenities and a choice of alternative routes if the climb up the Allt leaves you cold.

The lake itself is relatively low-lying, at just 154 metres above sea level and is fringed with over ten hectares of reed beds and rich grassland, as well as woodland dominated by alder and willow. This attracts a fantastic array of birds from great crested glebes and mute swans to Canada geese, moorhens, coots and curlews. It is also the second largest breeding site in

Wales for reed warblers and reed buntings as well as being an important habitat for thousands of starlings. It's not just a bird watchers' paradise in summer. Winter sees up to twenty or more different species arriving to feed at the lake including teal, tufted ducks and pochard. Even ospreys have been sighted here.

A walk around the lake itself is a good alternative to our route since the area offers the less adventurous visitor lots of facillities from a cafeteria to a caravan site! But however ambitious your walking plans are you shouldn't miss the Iron Age themed interpretation centre near the car park. Standing on stilts over the water, its roof rises like a witch's hat from among the reed beds, while the path to the hut is guarded by two imposing stone slabs. This startling little building is based on an Iron Age structure called a roundhouse and inside it offers beautifully framed vantage points onto the lake, as well as Llangorse's unique archaeological selling point, its crannog.

Derek's 'Harry Potter House' – the new interpretation centre at Llangorse Lake

Although these structures (mostly Iron Age) are quite plentiful in Scotland and Ireland this is the only one found in Wales and dates from the ninth century. It is a man-made island and is made out of rubble that was dropped into the water, behind an oak timber frame. In 916 AD the crannog was the scene of a daring raid by Ethelfled, Queen of Mercia and daughter of King Alfred. Ethelfled came to Wales on a revenge mission following the killing of an English priest and in an act of retribution she attacked the local kingdom of Brecheiniog and kidnapped the wife of Brychan, King of Brecheiniog, along with thirty-three of his followers. The captured Welsh were held prisoner on the crannog until Brychan finally managed to secure his wife's release.

The crannog is probably behind local folk tales which tell of a lost city that lies beneath the lake's surface (even though the deepest point of Llangorse measures just 8 metres). Legend has it that the ruler of this kingdom was a greedy and cruel princess who only agreed to marry a poor suitor after he promised her great wealth. In order to complete his end of the bargain, her husband-to-be robbed and murdered a rich merchant. But although his ill-gotten loot won him the hand of the princess, retribution was close at hand. The murdered man's ghost raised a terrible storm that flooded the city and created the lake.

In actual fact, Llangorse was created 12,000 years ago by glaciers during the last Ice Age. Despite the physical facts contradicting legend, our knowledge of the crannog is only relatively recent. Although maybe we shouldn't dismiss the myths so quickly. After all the crannog was only discovered in 1868 and in 1925 the waters here surrendered another find, a dug-out canoe that had been preserved in the mud since 800AD. So maybe there are still things in those shallow waters waiting to be uncovered.

If you do pop inside the visitor centre then look out of the shuttered window on your right and try and make out the route you're about to take. Just follow the line of the western end of the lake towards Tŷ Mawr farmhouse and then up above Llangasty before arriving at the ridge of Allt yr Esgair.

Leaving the crannog, you keep the lake to your left and head over the small bridge into open farmland. Within five minutes you will be heading out into quieter countryside, most of it agricultural land.

The first thing to keep your eyes peeled for is the smelly, sticky, boot-scraping evidence of the flocks of wild Canadian geese that live here. There can be around 500 geese feeding here at peak times, although the numbers that breed at Llangorse are fairly small. This itinerant mob of birds can provide a magnificent aerial display when taking off and then flying in their classic V-shaped formation with the dramatic scenery of the Beacons as their backdrop. On the ground however it's another story and the birds are very unpopular with the local farmers as they eat up and then fowl important pasture land. Coupled with the sheep and cattle that also graze on these fields, it means that you have to be careful where you step on this early part of the walk!

As the path continues inland and you leave the geese behind, you'll see some bizarre, stunted five-hundred-year-old oaks that look like seriously misguided attempts at bonsai trees. These are pollarded oaks, which have been continually pruned over hundreds of years. The top branches of these particular oaks have been regularly cut by farmers to use as timber or even cattle fodder, thus preventing the trees from reaching their full height while leaving the trunks to fatten and grow.

As you leave the oaks and lower farm fields you'll encounter some beautiful wild flower meadows that lead up towards the historic farmhouse at Tŷ Mawr. The fields here are managed by the National Park Authority for nature conservation – so even though the pasture here looks wild and overgrown it's actually a tightly controlled and maintained environment. It's still grazed by cattle but the real difference here is that the land has had no artificial fertiliser added to it – or any other kinds of chemicals.

As such the plant life here is far more diverse, creating a breeding ground for a variety of insects and in the summer, you'll see lots of butterflies and damsel flies lazily drifting along in the breeze. Often walkers will get hung up on looking for signs of mammals and reptiles while beneath their noses (and feet) there are so many interesting and varied kinds of invertebrates to be discovered and enjoyed.

One of the many conservation success stories here is the recent discovery of Two Tone Reed Beetles at the water's edge. Llangorse is the only site in Wales where these insects can be found and they had been thought to be almost extinct in Britain with just a few communities surviving in southern England. Plainly conservation work in the area is slowly paying off.

At the end of the meadow you arrive at Tŷ Mawr, the farm first seen from the crannog and the interpretation centre. This is a very old farm which is currently under restoration, although be aware that the building you see now is only a small part of the original structure. Originally this was the site of a medieval manor house but by the 1500s it had become a much larger residence called Tal-y-Llyn House which was three storeys high, with a large columned entrance.

In Elizabethan times the house was owned by Huw Powell, the Lord of Llangasty Tal-y-llyn who in 1584 was involved in a dispute with the other major landowner in the area, Blanche Parry, lady in waiting to Elizabeth I and keeper of the Queen's jewels. The dispute centred over fishing rights to the lake and who was best placed to take advantage of Llangorse's lucrative eel population. As part of the legal submissions, a map of the area was drawn with illustrations of the houses and the position of the all-important eel traps. Once lost and buried amongst ancient paperwork it now survives as a fascinating time capsule from Elizabethan Wales.

The house which stands on the site today, while a fine residence, is nowhere near the size and grandeur of Lord Powell's abode although it is a working farm and home to a fairly unique building service that provides specialist lime building materials for restoration projects. It's also the site of further archaeological work and throughout the year local schoolchildren come here to take part in a special dig run by the National

Park to excavate parts of the estate (the current project centres around an extension built in the 1700s).

As you leave the farm, the path follows the main road uphill and gets quite steep until it levels out at Llangasty village hall. Some walkers drop cars off here before embarking on the route, so that they can cut out a long walk back to the Lake at the walk's end. Others will simply bypass the first hour of this route, drive straight to the car park and then head up to the ridge, making it a quicker walk to the top and back.

Beyond the hall the path joins a track which pre-dates the Romans' arrival in Brecon, to a time when the Celtic tribes here used it as the main road down to the lake. The track is bowed and sunken through hundreds of years of use, with a steep-banked high hedgerow running alongside it. It's a track that runs right up to the Iron Age fort at the summit of the ridge, so you're climbing along a highway that's been in use for over 2,500 years.

When we walked it we weren't just following in the footsteps of those Ancient Britons but also a fox, whose pungent aroma hung muskily around the middle part of the track. As the path emerges from this corridor of hedgerow and banking, the views which make this walk so special begin to reveal themselves. As good as they are though don't linger too long over them. Instead keep pressing on towards the top of the ridge where the scenery will really blow you away.

After cutting through more hill pasture, you turn back into wooded scrubland, past the remains of an old hunting lodge, before emerging on the last stage of the climb to the top. It's at this point you get fantastic views of Pen y Fan to the south west, the Usk Valley and Builth Wells in the north west. Take a minute here to savour the panorama and again remind yourself that the best is still to come, before turning up the last hundred or so steep yards to the top.

The path here is at its most unfriendly with shoulder high bracken, nettles and thorny scrub. It's a haunt of yellowhammers, small thrush-like birds with a song that is said to sound like someone singing 'a little bit of bread and no cheese' – although we never heard it when we were here! As this rough, scratchy foliage begins to clear you find yourself on the ridge of Allt yr Esgair and in the middle of the remains of an Iron Age hill fort.

The ditch and earthworks here run around the outside of the ridge and are difficult to see, although the remains at the centre of the fort are much more visible – and much older. They are what's left of an earlier Bronze Age cairn, the burial place of a chieftain and one of many found at high points across the Beacons (there's one at Pen Y Fan for example). No one is sure whether these summit sites were chosen because they were closest to the sky or because they allowed these tribal chiefs – even in death – to stand guard over their people.

Stand in the middle of the fort and you are greeted with a 360 degree view that encompasses the Beacons, the Black Mountains, the Sugar Loaf, Waun Fach, Mynydd Llangorse, the Blorenge and the Llangattock Escarpment. It also gives you a bird's eye view of the lake and it's only when you get up high above the lie of the land that you can appreciate just how big it is. In fact it used to be much bigger and there is evidence to suggest that not long after it was formed it may have stretched as far as Bwlch and overflowed into the Usk valley. If you want to judge just how far that is then look out for Bwlch on the display board at the top of the ridge. The board also lists the mountains laid out before you and is a great help to the novice walker and to new visitors to the Park.

It's an amazing panorama with a real wow factor and on a clear day you'll feel like you've walked to the top of the world (although in truth you've climbed just over 1300 feet!) Once you've used up the space on your camera, head back down the way you came and get ready to show the pictures off, because this is a view that most of the visitors to Llangorse will never see or indeed ever know about. As such this route is a perfect way to end our year-long collection of walks and it encapsulates what we set out to do with *Weatherman Walking* – giving you a taste of these treasures hidden away in the wonderful Welsh landscape and encouraging you to go out and discover them for yourself.

Get Walking!

You've now got twelve good reasons to go walking in the great Welsh outdoors and follow in Derek's footsteps. But if you need even more encouragement to take part in Britain's most popular outdoor past time, consider these facts.

British walkers spend over £6 billion a year on their hobby and support some 245,000 full time jobs. During the same period, walker-related spending in Wales topped £132 million and generated 4,800 full-time jobs. Which is good but compared to what England and Scotland make out of walking, it's a case of 'could do better'. So how do we get a bigger slice of the pie?

Our situation would greatly improve if more Welsh people took up walking. The Scots for example, make a total of 300 million walking trips every year. That's a lot of snack bar business and car parking charges in anyone's money. And from a purely financial angle, putting public money into walking makes sense. For example, for every £1 spent on maintaining the Pembrokeshire Coastal path, £57 went back into the local economy – that's a pretty good return on the original investment. But let's not just dwell on the benefits walking brings to the business community alone, let's look at what it does for us as a nation.

Some experts believe that by promoting walking as an activity and encouraging more people to don Gore-Tex and sensible shoes, we could save the Health Service more than £7 billion a year. Barely 20% of people living in Britain get enough exercise to maintain a healthy lifestyle, while in Europe as a whole inactivity is a greater cause of illness than smoking. A brisk one mile walk completed in just 20 minutes will burn around 100 calories – which is the equivalent of 10 minutes of swimming or 16 minutes of aerobics. And unlike other forms of exercise, walking is free, requires no special equipment or training, and is a safe, low impact work out with a low risk of injuries and accidents. And as we've shown you, it can be done at all times of the year, allowing you to experience different surroundings in different seasons – and that's something which you shouldn't underestimate. All the evidence suggests that just spending time in the outdoors has a positive effect on your wellbeing and mental health. So walking gives you a healthy mind, a healthy body, it's good for the economy, and it's becoming more and more fashionable – even celebrities are doing it (well Derek does it anyway!). So walking gives you a healthy mind, a healthy body, it's good for the economy and not only that, it's becoming more and more fashionable – even celebrities are doing it (well Derek does it anyway!)

He's not alone. The average age of adults who regularly walk two or more miles for recreation is 43 and 77% of the UK's adult population (that's around 38 million people) admit to walking for pleasure at least once a month. Walkers are everywhere, they're getting younger and they're among the healthiest, happiest people in Britain. So skip back over the last couple of chapters and ask yourself this question – why wouldn't you want to spend a day walking in Wales?

So What's Next?

This book and the *Weatherman Walking* series make for a fine introduction to walking in Wales but if you're starting out, the best thing to do is contact your nearest National Park service or local walking club and join a guided group walk. Your local paper should carry contacts for walking groups but if not, you could try and find your nearest one by contacting the Ramblers Association at www.ramblers.org.uk.

Many local authorities do their bit to encourage walking too. Torfaen Council, for example, who promote the Iron Mountain Heritage trails at Blaenavon, advertise their own Community Health walks alongside their other Countryside events.

A quick Google around the internet will soon give you plenty of ideas about where to walk and although there are some excellent sites like www.walkingworld.com (where you can pay £1.50 and download a guided walk with an Ordinance Survey map and an easy to follow picture guide) there are lots of free sites with enough information to get you going. For example, the Wales Tourist Board offers a free Outdoor Activity guide on walking which you can order at www.visitwales.com. Log on to the BBC Wales Where I Live sites (at www.bbc.co.uk/whereilive) or the official *Weatherman Walking* site at www.bbc.co.uk/walesweather and again you'll find lots of free and useful information (not only that but you can also download your own little Desktop Derek there – now there's a treat!)

Your best source of walking knowledge and good advice, however, are the sites run by each of the individual National Parks. Click on www.breconbeacons.org for example and you'll get a full list of all their guided walks and seasonal events, while sites like www.nationaltrust.org.uk or the Snowdonia site at www.eryri-npa.co.uk will also lead you to a wealth of walking possibilities.

Finally, if the internet isn't your thing there are now lots of dedicated walking magazines around, although for one that's exclusively tailored to the Welsh market, order a copy of *Walking Wales*. It comes with lots of great walks with easy to follow maps and directions as well as some inspirational features on what makes Wales a walkers' paradise. The address for the magazine is, *Walking Wales*, 3 Glantwymyn Village Workshops, Glantwymyn, Machynlleth, Powys and it's available by subscription. One last piece of advice. If all else fails, ring your local Tourist Information centre. They're not just there for tourists and they could point you in the direction of some great little walks which are probably right under your feet.

So now you have everything you need to get you walking in Wales. Well perhaps not quite everything. After all there is one thing we all like to have when we're outdoors and that's good weather. And while we can't guarantee sunshine and blue skies, if you want the latest forecasts then check out Derek's regular broadcasts on BBC Radio Wales. You can find the station on 882 and 657 AM, 93 – 104 FM and satellite channel 0117.

Let's just hope that when you go walking he gets the forecast right!

Weatherman Walking is just one of a whole range
of Welsh-interest publications from Y Lolfa.
For a full list of publications,
ask for your free copy of our catalogue
– or simply surf into our secure website,
www.ylolfa.com
and order online.

TALYBONT, CEREDIGION, CYMRU (WALES), SY24 5AP
email ylolfa@ylolfa.com
website www.ylolfa.com
tel. (01970) 832 304
fax 832 782